W9-AQO-159

TWAYNE'S WORLD AUTHORS SERIES

A Survey of the World's Literature

Sylvia E. Bowman, Indiana University

GENERAL EDITOR

LATIN LITERATURE

Philip Levine, University of California

EDITOR

Petronius

(TWAS 97)

TWAYNE'S WORLD AUTHORS SERIES (TWAS)

The purpose of TWAS is to survey the major writers —novelists, dramatists, historians, poets, philosophers, and critics—of the nations of the world. Among the national literatures covered are those of Australia, Canada, China, Eastern Europe, France, Germany, Greece, India, Italy, Japan, Latin America, New Zealand, Poland, Russia, Scandinavia, Spain, and the African nations, as well as Hebrew, Yiddish, and Latin Classical literatures. This survey is complemented by Twayne's United States Authors Series and English Authors Series.

The intent of each volume in these series is to present a critical analytical study of the works of the writer; to include biographical and historical material that may be necessary for understanding, appreciation, and critical appraisal of the writer; and to present all material in clear, concise English—but not to vitiate the scholarly content of the work by doing so.

Petronius

By PHILIP B. CORBETT
University of Aberdeen

Twayne Publishers, Inc. :: New York

Library of Congress Catalog Card Number: 79-79217

MANUFACTURED IN THE UNITED STATES OF AMERICA

For Stévane

PETRONIUS

by

PHILIP B. CORBETT

This concise analytical study claims for itself a measure of originality. Its author is no stranger to his subject, having "taught" Petronius for many years and thought about him not a little.

In the past, Petronian scholarship has been most fruitfully concerned with elucidation of the text. The fragments are a rich field for the textual critic and many ingenious emendations adorn the various editions, particularly those of the last two centuries. In more recent times even more industry has been expended in categorizing the morphological and syntactical phenomena of Petronius' deliberately colloquial Latinity.

Literary appreciation of Petronius' work has had a less profitable run. Two major problems bedevil the critic; first, "What does the title *Satyricon* mean?" and secondly, "To what literary genre or genres does the work belong?".

The author attempts to deal with both these questions in his account of the incidents and characters of the *Satyricon*. The resulting subjective interpretation depends for its value upon what stimulus it may give to criticism and so to further elucidation of the Arbiter, his work and its place in world literature.

Preface

Factual information regarding Titus Petronius, "Arbiter of Elegance," is of the scantiest. An intimate friend of the Emperor Nero until he incurred the latter's enmity, he is, by the general consensus of scholars, author of the *Satyricon,* a work we possess in substantial fragments and which appears to be a burlesque entertainment composed to amuse the court circle.

The present study is divided into four chapters. The first gives a brief assessment of Petronius' character as revealed by Tacitus, and adds glimpses of personalities likely to have known and influenced our author. The second chapter examines the problem of the title *Satyricon* and hazards an explanation of it, in view of the literary elements to be found in the work. *Satyricon* appears to be for the delectation of *satyricoi* and so an attempt is made to identify them.

The third chapter analyzes the *Satyricon,* commenting on the genres involved. The fourth deals with Petronius' literary influence through the ages.

The Notes and Bibliography are designed to stimulate further investigation by interested readers into our author's life and work.

Background material is abundant and readily available for a study of the time of Nero, to which our author presumably belonged. It is not my purpose in this critical analysis of Petronius' work to draw largely upon this material. Where established facts are lacking, undue speculation may irritate. The *Satyricon* is a work puzzling in its unique nature and must to a considerable extent be allowed to speak for itself. I trust that the following pages enable it to do so.

My cordial thanks are due to Professor Philip Levine of the University of California at Los Angeles for the immense care he has taken in helping me to prepare my manuscript. My wife has supported me during its composition with constant encouragement. Mrs. Sheila Todd here in Aberdeen has been a most conscientious and efficient typist. I wish also to record my gratitude to Professor Sylvia Bowman, General Editor of the TWA Series, for welcoming me to an exciting new project.

P.B.C.

ABOUT THE AUTHOR

Philip B. Corbett is a Senior Lecturer in Humanity at the University of Aberdeen, Scotland. A graduate of Sheffield University with First Class Honours in French and in Greek and Latin, he gained his Doctorat en Philosophie et Lettres at Louvain in 1954 with "the highest distinction."

At Aberdeen, his teaching and research have been concerned with the colloquial Latin authors, both early and late. He is perhaps best known for his work on the Latinity of the early medieval period, particularly for his linguistic contribution to the diplomatic edition of the *Regula Magistri* (Paris, 1953) and for his *Latin of the Regula Magistri* (Louvain, 1958), a work well known to patristic scholars. Articles and reviews from his pen have appeared in *Scriptorium, Speculum, Moyen-Age, Revue d'Histoire et de Philologie, The Journal of Theological Studies, Studia Monastica, The New Catholic Encyclopedia, Romance Philology, Eranos* and *Classical Philology*.

In 1960, Dr. Corbett was invited to lecture at Ottawa University on Sallust, whose colloquialism he has closely studied, and on Medieval Latin Poetry. As Visiting Professor at the University of California at Los Angeles in 1964 he helped to establish there a new course in Medieval Latin.

Contents

Chronology

Conjectural, except for the date of death, given by Tacitus in *Annals,* 16.17.

A.D. 27 Approximate birth date[1] of Titus[2] Petronius.
60 Succeeded Tarquitius Priscus[3] as governor of Bithynia.
61 Consul suffectus in place of his brother Petronius Turpilianus,[4] summoned to take command of the Roman armies in Britain, until the appointment of the regular consul Publius Calvisius Ruso, who took office March 1, 61.
61 Height of Petronius' favor with Nero. Given the appellation Arbiter Elegantiae. Probable date of the *Satyricon.*
62 Appointment of Ofonius Tigellinus, Petronius' deadly enemy, as Commander of the Imperial Guard. Beginning of Petronius' decline in favor.
66 Petronius' disgrace and suicide.

CHAPTER 1

Petronius the Arbiter

I *Tacitus' Pen Portrait*

FEW present-day scholars doubt that the delightful entertainment called *Satyricon* was written in the middle of the first century of the Christian era. Content, style and, above all, atmosphere are completely in keeping with a period about which we know a great deal from contemporary documents, historical and literary, as well as from modern archeological and sociological investigation.[1]

By common consent, the author of this entertainment is one Petronius who, born in the reign of Tiberius, survived that of Claudius and died by his own hand in the year A.D. 66, as a consequence of incurring the disfavor of Nero. His portrait, briefly but vividly penned by the historian Tacitus some fifty years later, has, together with the *Satyricon* itself, so captured the imagination of all subsequent generations that Petronius is one of the best known figures of Latin literature.

In the sixteenth book of his *Annals* (chapters 17–19), Tacitus, describing the reign of terror of A.D. 66, following the discovery of Piso's alleged plot the previous year to overthrow Nero's régime, writes:

> Within the space of a few days there fell, like a line of soldiers in battle, Annaeus Mela, Anicius Cerialis, Rufrius Crispinus and Petronius—.
>
> Concerning the latter we must say a few words. He spent the daytime in sleep, reserving his nights for the duties and pleasures of life. With other men, it is industry which advances them to fame; in his case it was idleness. Yet he was not considered a glutton or a waster, like most people who exhaust their inheritance, but rather a refined practitioner of luxurious living. The freedom of his speech and conduct displayed a certain studied negligence of self and was the more welcomed for its appearance of honesty.
>
> All the same, as governor of Bithynia and then as consul, he showed

himself energetic and equal to the tasks of office. After this, he lapsed again into vice or at least an affectation of vice, and was admitted to the intimate circle of Nero's personal friends, in the capacity of Arbiter of Elegance. Indeed, the emperor considered nothing which had not been recommended to him by Petronius as likely to yield the pleasing sensuality required by luxurious living.

As a result, Tigellinus became jealous of Petronius as a rival and one superior to himself in the science of pleasure. And so he went to work upon the emperor's cruelty, the vice which in him prevailed over all others, accusing Petronius of being a friend of the conspirator Scaevinus. A slave was bribed to give information. No opportunity for defense was given and most of Petronius' servants were thrown into prison.

It so happened that at this time Nero had gone to Campania. Petronius followed him but, on reaching Cumae, was detained there. He decided not to linger on in either hope or despair. However, he did not immediately put an end to his life, but cut open his veins and then bound them up again, to open or close them at will, conversing the while with friends, but not upon serious matters nor seeking by his discourse to win glory in a display of stoicism. He listened instead while they sang lighthearted songs or delivered quantities of smooth-flowing verse. Upon some of his slaves he bestowed gifts, upon others a whipping. Finally, he installed himself at the dinner table and then relaxed in sleep, so that death, although deliberately sought, might appear fortuitous.

In his will, he did not, like the majority of those dying in such circumstances, flatter Nero, Tigellinus, or others in power. Instead, he wrote down an account of the emperor's debaucheries, together with the names of his associates therein, male and female, and the outrageous details of each type of perversion. This document he sealed with his signet ring and sent to Nero. Then he broke the ring, so that it might not be used again to cause trouble for others.

II *A Slender Dossier*

There is little enough on the purely factual side to be gleaned from the account just quoted, and yet it is rich in details of character and richer still in implications. To read it is to understand why all through the centuries people have been eager to identify the man of whom Tacitus here speaks with the author of the *Satyricon,* a work which, at least superficially, appears to be so much in keeping with the personality here revealed.

First then as to the bare facts: Petronius was a familiar of Nero, admitted to the circle of his intimate friends at court. He was a governor of Bithynia and later a consul, the dates we are not told. (See the Chronology and the Notes pertaining thereto.) The appellation Arbiter Elegantiae was bestowed upon him, presumably by the emperor himself, jestingly, but invested with the weight of his authority. The growing influence of Tigellinus, his rival postulant for the emperor's favor, finally brought about his downfall, culminating in suicide at Cumae, a protracted process in the grand manner during which our author penned an incriminating document against his erstwhile patron which was signed, sealed, and delivered.

Sparse information, but in keeping with the accompanying character sketch. Petronius, it seems, achieved actual fame by his way of life. He was not considered a debauchee and a waster, but a master of the art of living, to which he brought a sense of refinement and good taste. So says Tacitus, and while we must remain aware of the historian's ever-present irony, we must also bear in mind the standards of the world in which Petronius had his being. His speech and actions were of a studied laxity, and his disregard for personal reputation bore witness to a certain ingenuousness which won sympathy. However, this candor (*simplicitas*) was overlaid with a veneer of cynicism. By flouting convention and by the affectation of vice, Petronius sought to impose his personality at the court. He succeeded, so that in the matter of extravagant behavior Nero regarded him as a master.

But, in assessing the character of Petronius the playboy, we must recall that Tacitus described him as energetic and equal to his task both as provincial governor and as consul. Also, in the last hours of his life and the conduct of his self-imposed death, he displayed a gaiety and incongruity demanding a high degree of courage. From these things we must conclude that our author was a greater man than either his *simplicitas* or his cynicism implies. In the former quality, as we shall see, lies the secret of the interpretation of his written work, while his cynicism has its origin in a philosophy of life which was in vogue in his day for reasons we shall consider in the next chapter.

III *The Personal Background*

In the case of our author there are, so to speak, two backgrounds, both of which affect his life and work. The two merge inevitably, but are distinguishable, one from the other. They are the physical or personal background of contemporary society and events and the intellectual or literary background which is founded in a tradition.

The personal background is the more readily discernible and will be touched upon here, briefly, because its impact upon Petronius' work is superficial, though genuine. The literary background is more subtle and of fundamental importance for the appreciation of the *Satyricon.* It will be dealt with in the next chapter.

The curse of the society to which our author belonged was its leisure. Considerable will-power and zest for life were needed to make a young man, possessed of enormous material resources, whose slightest physical needs were catered for by hosts of slaves, to bestir himself to industrious behavior in the service of the State or of his fellow men. Strong ambition, liking for power, and responsibility were necessary, and Petronius did not possess these qualities sufficiently. Furthermore, under the early emperors, Tiberius, Caligula, Claudius, and Nero, all tyrants of unbalanced and capricious conduct, more than mere ambition was required. It took no small courage to work at a political career, where emergence into prominence was fraught with daily peril of the tyrant's disfavor, incurred directly or through the intrigues of lesser men, the informers, that notorious band whose activities were the plague of the age. The pages of Tacitus and Suetonius are a grim and monotonous recital of atrocities and murders resulting from such delation, removing now this, now that important figure from the political scene because of real or presumed danger to the imperial status quo.

It is true that Petronius did not lack courage. Indeed, he displayed it, not only in the manner of his self-inflicted death, carried out with dignity and even gaiety, but also in the novelty of his chosen way of life, pursued with evidence of determination and vigor. But mundane ambition and a desire for that posthumous fame so dear to most Romans were not his. The *cursus honorum* was open to him as a *fils de famille* and he went through it as a matter of course and with efficiency, gaining thereby the necessary social cachet. His heart was not in it.

The profession of oratory, the alternative to and, in the case of outstanding men, the concomitant of a political career, was equally open to Petronius. It too was not without danger. Seneca's success as an orator almost cost him his life under the madman

Caligula whose jealousy he thereby incurred. Judging from Petronius' facility of style, we cannot doubt that he could have achieved fame as a public speaker, had he so wished. Apparently, he did not.

It is clear that he who became the Arbiter of Elegance had what is called the artistic temperament. He possessed the culture and refinement of the artist to a superlative degree, together with the excessive delicacy and sensitivity which often accompany them. A certain weakness of disposition disinclined him to the sustained effort required for a successful political or oratorical role. Certainly he was eager to play a significant part in an enclosed society and in this he was successful. He devoted his great talents to living a highly unconventional life. This brought him an equally unconventional success and the kind of popularity he desired within an exalted and exclusive circle of acquaintance.

But he achieved far more than this. He applied himself to an unconventional, in many ways unique, form of literature, achieving a deserved success and a lasting fame such as he could not have foreseen. At the same time he avoided any kind of writing which might have made him suspect, whether history, oratory, or philosophy. His position about the throne might have induced him to epic, but no doubt he disdained to glorify a régime he knew to be corrupt and degenerate.

The hypersensitive and introspective artist in Petronius forbade him to seek the limelight as a public orator or politician. Perhaps also his sensuality and cynicism imposed upon him a certain prudence and reserve, that he might continue to enjoy a favor and a reputation most congenial to his temperament.

In avoiding the life of sustained public service to which his status invited him, the Arbiter was not altogether unrepresentative of the society in which he moved. He was what we nowadays call an escapist. By his withdrawal from the day-to-day activity of public and even of private life, since, if we are to believe Tacitus, he spent much of the daytime in sleep, he entered upon a nighttime existence which of necessity must have had little or no concern with the normal activities and pastimes of other men—the round of the Forum, consultations with lawyers, politicians, and bankers, with teachers of rhetoric and philosophy. He cannot have exercised in the gymnasia and wrestling schools, listened to recitals of music and verse, in normal hours with most of his contemporaries. He may or may not have held a morning levee to listen to the desires and complaints of clients, but he can hardly have bestirred himself to act personally on their behalf. He can hardly have frequented the public games, racing contests, gladiatorial combats, animal baiting, the massacre of Christians and criminals, the theatrical performances, acrobats and tight-rope walkers, all of which formed the regular program of public entertainment.

This withdrawal was deliberate. The escapist mood sought only those companions and entertainments which fastidious choice dictated. Night life is vigorous and varied enough in a Mediterranean climate. Outdoor feasting and merrymaking, singing, dancing, drinking, and bathing are enlivened by torch light. The streets are clearer for sallying forth to acts of vandalism and debauchery which are best conducted in semi-obscurity. We may be sure that Petronius found kindred spirits to accompany him. But to make such conduct habitual betrays a mind which seeks to escape from the normal and denotes a certain malaise characteristic of an age frustrated by the fetters of tyranny. There were not a few in the days of Nero who felt freer to express themselves under cover of darkness, not least they who dwelt closest to the source of their disquiet. It was an age which, without knowing it, was ready to receive the new message of hope for mankind which was beginning to find its way among those classes of society remotest from that in which our author had his being.

Petronius, the sensitive artist, sought partial escape then in an unconventional mode of existence, shared no doubt by a few like-minded spirits. It is probable that this disregard for convention was not least of the traits which attracted Nero's sympathetic attention to him, for was he not himself an artist? Of this, more presently.

But our author was no recluse, as his influential role at court proves. On the contrary, he was extremely good company, an agreeable and witty companion, full of novel ideas.

It is not possible, from perusal of either Tacitus' account of him or of the *Satyricon,* to fit him into any of the political events of the time. There is no evidence that he was actually involved in Piso's conspiracy of the year 65, although his enemy Tigellinus attempted to involve him by pointing out his friendship with Scaevinus, a leading conspirator. Neither do we hear, on the social side, of any scandal with any of the women at court, not even the profligate Messalina of fatal fascination.

We must limit our remarks to people who must inevitably in some way have influenced Petronius, because we know that they came into contact with him and that their lives were in varying degree bound up with his. They constitute his immediate background and its atmosphere. I shall mention five such people, of whom one was, of course, the emperor himself, in a sense the Arbiter's *raison d'être* and a decisive influence upon his creative activity. Of the other four, two were companions of his pleasures and vices, the third perhaps a power for good, the fourth his destroyer.

IV *The Lady Silia*

The two companions were Scaevinus and the wife of a senator, Silia. She is the one woman whose name we may closely link with that of Petronius. Tacitus tells us that she was a great friend of our author (*Annals,* 16.20.1). So much so that Nero, wondering how on earth the Arbiter could have found out the lurid details of his most secret debaucheries written up in the damning document forwarded from the death bed at Cumae, thought of her as the informant. Thus we know that Petronius' loyalty to Silia forbade him to mention her name. But it had to be someone with inside knowledge, and Silia had been a willing participant with Nero in the most daring profligacies the pair of them had been able to think up. And so he banished her into exile because she had not kept her mouth shut.

What concerns us for the Petronius picture is his close friendship with the lady. She may have been one of innumerable mistresses of his; she may have been his one true love who took refuge in his company when bored or disgusted with the emperor. In either case she links Petronius with the purely licentious element of the court life, proving that the cynical esthete did not live wholly upon an intellectual plane, affecting a lofty disdain of more brutish elements of the society for whom he was the exemplar of refinement. To be sure, we never think of Petronius as a prude and indeed he could not have been if he were to hold the affection of Nero, but it is good to know that he did not dislike women, nor they him. We are grateful to Tacitus for his brief allusion to the friendship of Petronius and Silia.

V *The Conspirator*

Now a word about Scaevinus, already mentioned above.

Flavius Scaevinus[2] was, like Petronius, of senatorial rank and probably also at one time a member of the court circle. His way of life in some ways resembled that of Petronius, being devoted to the pleasures of this world. Tacitus tells us that he had enfeebled his mind by excess and was of slothful disposition. Presumably he lacked the energy and the artistry of our author.

Nero had somehow offended him, for he displayed a savage mood in entering upon the conspiracy centered about Piso's name, claiming the privilege of striking the first blow at the emperor when he should be seated at the circus games in honor of Ceres on April 12, 65. To this end he had removed a sacrificial knife from a temple to Fortuna in Etruria. The foolish man made much of this acquisition and on returning home, ordered it to be sharpened by his freedman Milichus, who lost no time in reporting the incident to Nero himself. Scaevinus was arrested, together with another conspirator, Antonius Natalis, and the two of them confessed and revealed the names of others involved, including the philosopher Seneca and the poet Lucan.

Tacitus' stirring pages of these incidents and their sequel speak eloquently of the atmosphere of hatred and distrust, panic and savagery, extravagance and heroism which those near to the emperor, including our Petronius, breathed in the darkening days of the tyrant's decline. This was the background of his daily existence against which he jested and entertained and wrote his enduring contribution to the world's literature.

Scaevinus, his chosen companion of temperamental affinity, unwittingly encompassed the Arbiter's doom, wrought at the hands of him whom we shall next consider, Gaius Ofonius Tigellinus,[3] the vilest representative of a vile period of history.

VI *The Horse Dealer*

He was the shady son of a shady father, a Sicilian living in exile in Southern Italy. Somehow he arrived in the household of Nero's father, Cnaeus Domitius, made the acquaintance of the future emperor, and committed adultery with Agrippina, Domitius' wife and Nero's mother. He also spent some time in the service of Marcus Vinicius, consul in 30 and in 45, long enough to have an affair with Vinicius' wife, Julia Livilla, daughter of Drusus Germanicus, grand-daughter of Tiberius, sister of Gaius. From which we see that his ambitions ran high and that he had some kind of ruthless charm. His licentious activities, however, resulted in his banishment by Gaius in 39.

He was recalled but kept quiet under Claudius (41–54), who, for all his eccentricities, was a serious-minded man, not likely to be interested in what Tigellinus had to offer, riotous and brutal horseplay, both literal and figurative. For apparently he renewed his friendship and favor with Claudius' successor Nero, as the result of his horse-breeding activities, since the young emperor was especially keen on equestrian pursuits, above all chariot racing, which had a great vogue in his reign.

We are not concerned with the appalling details, familiar to readers of Tacitus, of Tigellinus' career of cruelty and delation, of his fiendish determination to secure absolute dominion over Nero's personality and to direct his vacillating policies. One by one he removed from his master's entourage all possible rivals for popular or senatorial favor. The conspiracy of Piso gave him a glorious opportunity to exterminate by torture and murder many scions of illustrious houses, thereby paying off personal scores against those who despised his humble origin and, at the same time, keeping alive Nero's ever-present fears and suspicions by alluding to fresh dangers arising from the continued existence of this or that personage.

What does concern us is the fact that by the year 62 Tigellinus had reached a position of great power, that of one of the two commanders of the Imperial Bodyguard, the *corps d'élite* whose caprice had placed Claudius upon the throne, on whose goodwill Nero depended for his continued tenure of the same, whose support would decide his successor. It is probable that the death of the honest soldier Burrus,[4] which made possible the sinister advent to his vacant post, was contrived by our horse fancier. At any rate, Burrus' demise removed one of the two forces for good which had been responsible for a beneficent control of Nero's activities. The other force, Seneca, was now irretrievably impaired. The brilliant philosopher, businessman, educator, and administrator must seek retirement. His doom is close at hand.

The acquisition by Tigellinus of this supremely important post meant immediate disaster for Petronius. From this moment onwards he could no longer be sure of his position at court. His rival set to work to undermine his influence. How could he now continue to have the emperor's ear in all that concerned pleasurable living? The Sicilian held in contempt the refinement and artistry of the Arbiter and was for helping Nero to improve his wrestling style and his dashing performance as a charioteer rather than to get his approval for tonight's menu or a turn of phrase for an epigram. The year 62 was the effective end of a brief splendor in the arbitration of elegance, which presumably did not begin until Petronius' return from Bithynia at the end of 60. It is perhaps in the middle of this little heyday, say in 61, that we should place the composition of the *Satyricon*,[5] intended as it surely was for the entertainment of a circle of intimates as yet unsullied by the presence of a brutal antagonist whose sneers would blight its reception by him for whom it was chiefly conceived.

VII *The Power for Good*

The chief influence upon Nero's formative years was a beneficent one, that of the distinguished philosopher, savant, and man of the world, Lucius Annaeus Seneca.[6] Nero was barely twelve years old when, in 49, his mother Agrippina, anxious to secure goodwill for him whom she destined for the throne, recalled Seneca from exile in Corsica and appointed him the boy's tutor. Not only Nero, however, but the whole of the upper-class society of Rome came under the Spaniard's eloquent spell. His nicely balanced philosophy of Stoic practical wisdom, self-control and constancy in misfortune, combined with Epicurean fearlessness of death and freedom from superstition, was admirably suited to the needs of an age of uncertainty and violence. Indeed, there is more than a hint in Seneca's insistent declamations, rising not infrequently to a ranting, almost hysterical fervor, of the escapist note which characterizes the nervous thinking of a tyrant-ridden society.

The theoretical calm of Seneca's teaching of reasoned morality and virtue in harmony with Nature is transcended in the high-flown outbursts of distraught passion in his tragedies. The regal state is fraught with fear and Thyestes suddenly longs for the peace of the poor man's cottage, the security of his humble table. The rhetoric-laden verse of Seneca's nephew, Lucan, betrays the same restless uneasiness underlying the Stoic fervor of his moralizing, the leaven of his uncle's teaching.

But what of Petronius? Can there be a greater contrast between the cynical hedonism of his writing and the incessant preaching of Seneca's often tiresome moral tirades? We can plainly see Seneca in Lucan, but where is he in Petronius?

Certainly we find traits of the Senecan philosophy in Petronius' way of life. The indulgent attitude towards human shortcomings, a fatal flaw in Seneca's authority over the young Nero, is everywhere apparent in the *Satyricon*. Ultimately, Seneca is agnostic; he cannot define the nature of the power which created and then let down mankind. Petronius is of course no philosopher himself, still less a theologian. His gods, mentioned casually in satiric vein, are mostly the swayers of the passions, Venus and her grotesque son, Priapus. Fortuna he recognizes for her fickle self. Petronius fled the light of day, disgusted with the triviality of everyday events, into a serene interior existence where escape was more possible from the fetters of responsibility.

He pursued knowledge and refinement as Seneca pursued them, but without the philosopher's firm intention to fortify his spirit with their moral implications. Petronius thinks along the same lines as Seneca, but lacks his moral conviction. It is this lack of moral purpose which is the chief characteristic of Petronius' writing, whereas it is everywhere manifest in Seneca. The Spaniard's message failed with our author, as it failed with Nero. But Petronius did not succumb to the basest passions as did Nero. His delicacy of temperament saved him from the gross degeneracy we witness in the emancipated emperor.

The manner of Petronius' death is perfectly in accord with Senecan Epicurean-flavored Stoicism. Death is either the beginning of non-existence or the entry to a happier world, it matters not which. In either case it is to be taken lightly, a subject for jest.

Seneca the man loved power and entered politics to help him to achieve it. But his true sage avoids public life and Nero's minister came to regret the part he had chosen for himself and to seek retreat, a delayed practitioner of his own preaching. Petronius already possessed the wealth which Seneca had to acquire before he could permit himself to despise it. Too late did the older man follow the younger in fleeing the world's entanglements.

In weariness of his surroundings, Petronius turned to study the life of the common man. The aim of his book, he tells us, is to record something new and sincere (*novae simplicitatis opus*), the activities of ordinary folk (*quodque facit populus, candida lingua refert,—Satyricon,* 132. 15).

Both Seneca and Lucan profess sympathy for the humble condition, since Stoicism declares a contempt for corporal pleasures and possessions which hinder the pursuit of virtue by fettering the spirit. Thyestes' "Crime does not enter a cottage" (*scelera non intrant casas,—Thyestes,* 451) is echoed in Lucan's splendid eulogy of poverty on the occasion of Caesar's visit to a poor fisherman (*Pharsalia* V, 513 f.). Poverty is also the lot of Encolpius and his companions in their wanderings which are the tale of the *Satyricon.* There is every indication that they prefer their vagrant condition to the assumption of the responsibilities of stability. They have an independence which Petronius portrays with sympathy. It is forbidden to him by his exalted position in court society.

There can be no doubt that Petronius came under the spell of Seneca, like those around him. To read his work in the light of Seneca's compromise between Stoicism and Epicureanism is to discern elements of the philosopher's thought in one who had little use for philosophy as such, but who reflects the desire to escape into an unconfined world of the spirit, where even morality has no place. Here, Petronius goes beyond Seneca, whose work is permeated with incessant moral purpose to free Man's mind for virtue. Seneca's life fell short of its avowed purpose of spiritual freedom. That of Petronius also fell short of such freedom and was without avowed purpose. But his principal characters, Encolpius and Eumolpus, although beset with what are to them very real misfortunes, treated comically for our amusement, achieve a measure of freedom, at least on the physical plane befitting their humble status, denied to the tutor-minister of Nero and to the Arbiter of Elegance, who, in their different ways, pursued this least accessible commodity of their environment.

Petronius made a study of the style of Seneca. His smooth-flowing, sparkling, and subtle quality and many of his turns of phrase recall the brilliant essayist. Furthermore, there are many echoes of Seneca in our author which appear to be a parody of the philosopher's views.[7] Not least, there is the same satiric verve, the same eye for human foibles, the coquetry of women, the gluttony of men, the same ready wit to coin a pun or an epigram to point an observation.

I have called Seneca a force for good upon Petronius, a formative influence upon an alert and sensitive artist. That is so, even though the Arbiter occasionally makes fun of the older man, an early indication perhaps of Seneca's waning prestige at court.

VIII *Nero the Artist*

"What an artist is dying!" was Nero's remark while, at his order, a few faithful companions dug a grave for him at the villa of a freedman favorite in the suburbs of Rome as he awaited sentence of death (Suetonius, *Nero*, 49). The words sum up his chief ambition in life and his own attitude regarding its fulfillment.

Nero's interest in literature and art was lifelong and genuine. The theatrical instinct was strong in him, and he was passionately concerned to display his talents to the world. Wedded to this instinct was his yearning for popular acclaim, and all our evidence reveals that he worked long and earnestly to achieve it.

Perhaps the feeling of insecurity which always haunted him and led to some of his worst crimes urged him to seek the support of the masses. Had not Messalina tried to have him strangled in his cradle? (Suetonius, *Nero*, 6).

His passion for public spectacles was partly inherited. His father, Cnaeus Domitius, when consul, had provided beast baitings and gladiatorial shows, infamous for their cruelty (also a predominant trait in the son) and had compelled Roman knights and matrons to act in scurrilous mimes.

From boyhood, the future emperor had evinced two major interests—horsemanship and the theater arts. In the circus at the secular games of 47 before the reigning Claudius, he, then a boy of ten, took part on horseback with young Britannicus, the heir, in a mock battle of Troy, to the applause of the common people who took him to their hearts. The experience was never forgotten, and always Nero prided himself as horseman and charioteer, giving frequent displays of his skill in public. Small wonder that the evil Tigellinus, himself a horse fancier, saw in this penchant the way to assure his eventual domination over Nero.

But it is the artistic, not the equestrian side of the emperor's nature which concerns us, for this is where Petronius will come in. A word or two then about this aspect.

He was only sixteen when he sought distinction as an orator before the Senate. Seneca had of course trained him in the art of speaking, in which he was himself so accomplished. He pleaded on behalf of the people of Troy that they might be relieved of tax contributions to the Roman exchequer. The cause of the traditional founders of Rome was and remained dear to him. Was not Aeneas the founder of the Julian line and so (by adoption) Nero's own forbear? This gave divine origin to the Imperial House, since Aeneas was the son of Venus, and no one was ever more convinced of divine attributes than Nero.

Another great supporter of Troy was Apollo, and Nero seems to have regarded himself as a reincarnation of the god, endowed with his talents as poet, musician, and patron of the arts in general. Nero's flatterers encouraged the view and Seneca, in his satire on the death of Claudius, makes Apollo say "he is like me in the beauty of his looks and not inferior in his singing voice" (*Ludus de Morte Claudi,* 4.1). Nero dutifully strove to live up to the likeness and practiced constantly upon the lute, Apollo's instrument, also taking great pains to improve his voice which was somewhat weak, Suetonius tells us. The historian gives an amusing account of how Nero used to lie upon his back with a leaden plate upon his chest, purge himself with a syringe and with vomiting and avoid injurious foods (Suetonius, *Nero,* 20).

He also wrote verse, including a poem on the capture of Troy, and played before crowded audiences parts from tragedy, mime, and dance. His exhibitionism caused him to inaugurate two new sets of games, the Iuvenalia in 59 and the Neronia in 60. In spite of the opposition of advisers, he was determined to play an active part in all kinds of popular entertainment, not only acting, singing, dancing, and playing on the lyre and flute, but also chariot driving and wrestling which he practiced assiduously. After all, Apollo was also the Sun-god who drove his chariot across the sky.

Always this self-chosen role of Apollo on earth was foremost in his mind, and eventually he had statues erected of himself in the guise of Apollo the Lutist. He contemplated a tour of Greece, to culminate in performances at the Olympic Games, the Greeks alone being really worthy of his talents. Meanwhile, on one occasion, at Naples, predominantly a Greek city, the theater collapsed shortly after he had sung there. No one was hurt. What greater proof of divine favor? Nero composed an ode to celebrate his preservation for greater things.

It is this preoccupation with the theater arts which is the key to the rapprochement between the emperor and his Arbiter.

Nero was of course the acknowledged leader of whatever literary coteries sprang up about him in response to his artistic temperament. Petronius was for some two years, 61 and 62, immediately following his governorship and consulship and until Tigellinus came to decisive power, the trusted adviser in all matters related to refined living. Such living, set within the décor of flagrant immorality and gross extravagance which the royal descendant of Venus considered appropriate to his earth-bound status, centered about a less unworthy core of intellectual activity for which, as kinsman and votary of Apollo, he felt himself divinely destined.

The Arbiter of Elegance shared with his master both the setting and the substance, designing his life to accord with interests at once congenial to his own temperament and dictated by circumstances. During his brief sway as Arbiter, our author both influenced the emperor and was influenced by him, and the very nature of his appointment as guide and counselor of Nero's leisure proves the unanimity of their artistic preoccupations.

The composition of the *Satyricon* to my mind belongs to this period of Petronius' arbitrage. It is the purpose of the next chapter to examine the traditional background of the work in terms of the various literary canons and conventions which contribute to its makeup. The third chapter will attempt to reveal the presence of this traditional background in an analysis of the *Satyricon.*

The latter was written as an entertainment for the court circle. Its considerable length, as estimated from the substantial fragments we possess, indicates that it was designed for reading in serial form at successive settings of a literary salon. The nature of its contents reveals certain themes in vogue in the first century, which I shall discuss later. It is sufficient to say here that in the pursuit of those themes Nero and Petronius had a common interest. This interest constitutes the *raison d'être* of the work. Had the *Satyricon* not conformed to Nero's tastes and artistic preoccupations, it would not have been written.

One aspect of the work may be mentioned here, since it reflects a trait of the emperor's character to which I have already referred

—his sympathy for the masses whose support and affection he craved, especially as an artist, from a sense of insecurity in his lofty eminence. Tyrants often have this craving in their dangerous isolation, deprived as they are of the love of those who have reason to hate them. As a young child Nero had known straitened circumstances and, by the irony of fate, his last hours were spent in destitution, abandoned by his courtiers, barefoot and almost in rags, with only a mattress for his bed. It is noteworthy that, upon his succession, acclaimed by the Guard and the Senate, he had refused but one of the honors showered upon him, that of Father of his Country, citing his youth as a pretext. The title meant something to him and he did not wish it carelessly bestowed upon one who had not yet deserved it.

Now it is not the least important of the many unique features of the *Satyricon* that it has for its theme the activities of ordinary folk. Petronius himself declares that its novelty lies in the candid presentation of the lives and loves of the commons. This novelty must have been of a kind likely to appeal to the emperor, or its author would not have conceived it for his pleasure. The characters depicted in the work are almost all of Greek or Near Eastern origin and are now settled in Campania; Nero had a special affection for the Greeks.

Like Petronius, he was a frequent visitor to the pleasant coastal resorts of Campania, where indeed he made his debut as a singer in public. The wealthy freedmen and their grotesque, extravagant behavior were as familiar to him as to our author. The prototypes of the guests at Trimalchio's table were almost certainly actual people known to Nero no less than to Petronius. The original of Trimalchio himself may have been a freedman formerly in the service of Petronius, although for the purpose of the story he is described as formerly belonging to one Pompeius, a common name in Campania, who purchased him from a Maecenas, the name of a family, like the Petronii, owning estates in Egypt.

The thread which runs through the *Satyricon* and makes it, among other things, a picaresque novel, is the narrative of the adventures of two students, Encolpius and Ascyltos, and their more elderly companion, Eumolpus. The various episodes which make up this narrative fall within well defined cadres of the Latin popular humorous tradition and embrace all the elements of the Roman inheritance of the Greek *palaestra,* the world of rhetoric, poetry, music and drama, folklore and romance, the world, in short, of the theater arts.

This world is that which Nero, as Apollo's votary, chose to study and with which he actively associated himself. Petronius is linked with him in this association as guide and companion. The entertainment he provided in response to his master's enthusiasm must be studied in this light, its background explained, its detail examined.

CHAPTER 2

Petronius the Satyricos

I *The Title of the Book*

PETRONIUS wrote a book called *Satyricon*. What does this title mean?

The earliest and best manuscript of the work, the ninth-century Berne codex,[1] has preserved the word in its original Greek form, not that with a Latinized ending (*satyricum*) which we sometimes meet with in the late Imperial grammarians.[2] *Satyricon* is the neuter form of the Greek adjective *satyricos,* derived from *satyros,* "a Satyr" and means "Satyr-like" or "pertaining to Satyrs." Neuter adjectives in both Greek and Latin can be used substantivally, but the Latinized *satyricum* usually occurs as an adjective, not as a substantive.

Satyricon, as applied to our author's work, is a substantive (= Latin *satyricum opus*) and means "a work in the Satyr vein or tradition." We have now to consider what Petronius, and we shall assume that he is responsible for the title, intended to convey by this.

The author himself tells us that the general theme of his book is the activities of ordinary folk, their lives and loves, treated with simplicity and candor. He also asks that prudes and ascetics withhold their criticism. In yielding to the joys which Venus prompts, we obey the behest of the father of truth, Epicurus himself, who declares such to be the purpose of life (132.15).

But there is not only simplicity and candor in Petronius' treatment. There is also satire,[3] although it is not of the malicious, carping nature to which we are accustomed in the chief exponents of the satirical genre in Latin literature. The Arbiter's satire is good-humored and tolerant, showing a new spirit, rather like that of Horace but even kinder and altogether devoid of moralizing. It is nevertheless there and must be taken into account in assessing the term *satyricon* which embraces it.

Petronius' *Satyricon* is something unique in Latin, indeed in world literature. In form only does it yield to a convention, that of the so-called Menippean satire, named after one Menippus of Gadara, a Cynic of the third century B.C. who gave humorous treatment to philosophy and who interspersed his prose with verses. The Romans took to this form of writing and among the lost works of the encyclopedist Marcus Terentius Varro (116–27 B.C.) are one hundred and fifty books of Menippean satires attacking the follies of his fellow men. The only extant Menippean of the classical period other than Petronius' work is the lampoon on Claudius commonly attributed to Seneca, in which the satire is extremely cruel and totally unlike that of our author.

Within this conventional framework of a mixture of prose and verse, Petronius presents us with what is in effect a kind of novel in the form of a narrative of the disreputable adventures of a dissolute young student Encolpius and the equally reprehensible characters he meets up with in the course of a vagrant existence. Thus we are confronted with something akin to that genre which in later ages is called picaresque. In actual fact, the nearest thing in spirit to the *Satyricon* is Voltaire's *Candide*. The acid Frenchman is almost a reincarnation of Petronius; certainly he is more biting, but he shares the exuberance and zest of the Roman, and Petronius found his most ardent and perceptive admirers among the cynical libertines of eighteenth-century France.

The *Satyricon* is a burlesque of humanity, a caricature of its absurdities, the vanity, ignorance, stupidity, greed, hypocrisy, extravagance, bad taste, and lasciviousness of men and women. Most of the characters belong to the lower orders, but among the more important are those who, like Encolpius, have pretensions to education and culture, but find themselves, perhaps from choice, living an unsettled existence on the fringe of society and subject to the vicissitudes of this condition.

How then does the word *satyricon* come to embrace such activities, treated with tolerant satire? How is such material in the Satyr tradition?

II *The Satyrs*

To answer these questions we must ask another: Who are the Satyrs?

They are the mythical attendants of a fertility god, personified in ritual drama from the dawn of classical literature and persisting in a tradition long after their actual dramatic role had ceased.

Man's greatest and most constant need is food. Only when this is assured him, can he turn his thoughts and actions to whatever other things are required to maintain and further his existence. From time immemorial the husbandman has felt his deepest satisfaction in the gathering-in of a good harvest, his keenest sorrow when there was little or none to gather. A successful harvest is a matter for rejoicing in the whole community and calls for celebration. Having toiled the whole year through at the seasonal tasks in heat and cold, rain and drought, the farmers and their womenfolk can now relax with the harvest in and make merry.

The poets of antiquity often tell of the rejoicings of country people at harvest time and we learn how the rustic communities of Greece and Italy came together for song and dance, music and jest on such occasions.[4] The keynote of their festivity is the gratitude they feel to the guardian spirits of Nature, the promoters of growth and fruitfulness and to the divinity they sense in the very products themselves, the hay and corn, wine and oil, and not less in the cattle, sheep, goats, and horses they have been able to rear and feed from the land.

The animal world is more visibly and tangibly alive than the abstract spirit world of mountain and stream, wind and rain, woodland and pasture. Thus we find mentioned in literature and depicted on vases and frescoes scenes of merrymaking in which human figures dance and gesticulate in the guise of goat and horse. They are the physical attendants of the more abstract fertility gods upon whom men and animals alike depend for their existence.

Among such half-human, half-animal representations are the Satyrs. By historical times they had become chiefly known as forming the chorus of a type of ritual known as the Satyr play,[5] whose characteristic is to parody themes drawn from mythology, providing light relief after the performance of tragedy at the spring festivals at Athens in honor of Dionysus, originally a fertility god but now more closely associated with the vine.

At the earlier Dionysiac festivals Satyrs appear to have worn horse ears and tails, but in later representations of them, as upon the Naples satyr-play vase,[6] they are habitually dressed in goat skins, whether from their association with tragedy (literally "goat song") or, more probably, because of their assimilation in tradition with the Arcadian Pan, the herdsman god of a region whose characteristic animal is the goat and who is therefore conceived with goatlike attributes.

What concerns us in all this is that goatishness came to be the distinctive mark of the Satyr in the tradition which attached to his name and to its derivatives and which persisted even after the disappearance of the Satyr chorus of ritual drama.

The goat is a playful, aggressive, and lascivious animal and as such is a commonplace of classical literature. The Satyr is accordingly vested with these characteristics and comes to represent the mischievous and wanton spirit in human nature.

Roman literary tradition adopted the Satyr along with so much else the Romans took from Greece. In addition to his wanton aggressiveness they imparted to him a further quality, which in satyr drama he may already have possessed, that of a sharp-tongued jester.

Words like *protervus* ("wanton"), *petulcus* ("aggressive") and *dicax* ("sharp-tongued") are stock epithets for the Satyr in Roman poetry.[7]

The primitive peoples of Italy had their own guardian and fertility spirits, among them Faunus, whose attendants, the Fauns, came to be identified with the Satyrs, so that the latter's goat attributes were bestowed upon the Italian spirits also. Faunus was vested with oracular powers, implicit in the epithet Fatuus ("the speaker") applied to him. In all probability the mordant, jesting tendency of the Satyroi-Fauni, their *dicacitas,* derives from their articulate role as Fatui, an important development for the satyric tradition reflected in Petronius' work. For this specifically Italian *dicacitas* is inherent also in a genre which the Romans prized as indigenous to themselves, the *satura.*

III Satura

It is not surprising that confusion should have arisen over the Greek *satyros* and its derivatives and the Latin word *satura.*[8] The close resemblance in form between them induced early grammarians to identify them etymologically, that is to say they derived *satura* from *satyros.* Thus, the fourth-century Diomedes, while giving a choice of possible derivations for *satura,* lists as number one "*satura* is so called from the Satyrs, because in this kind of poem laughable and shameful things are related in the same way as those uttered and performed by the Satyrs." [9]

It is not impossible that the Greek and the Latin words are in some way akin. *Satur* (*−a, −um*) means "full," "sated," and satiety is just what satyr celebrations are about, the repletion promised by the harvest. The second derivation offered by Diomedes is in keeping with this notion—*satura* refers to a dish (*lanx satura*) laden with a variety of first fruits and offered to the gods. The other two derivations are elaborations of the second—a kind of stuffing with many ingredients, or a bill (*lex satura*) including several provisions to be submitted for approval *en bloc.*

Whichever of these suggestions is the most correct and whether or no *satura* is connected with *satyros,* the fact remains that the Roman satire genre which they called *satura* is bound up with the satyric tradition. The humor of the Satyrs' merrymaking as perpetuated at Rome is strongly dosed with the bite of satire, that characteristic of the carping Latin temperament. This satirical element, though nicely restrained, is present in Petronius' *Satyricon,* along with the other ingredients inherent in its background, and, as we have noted, the form of his work is that of the *satura Menippea.*

IV *The Satyricoi*

Before considering the various ingredients of the *Satyricon,* a word must be said concerning the *satyricoi,* among whom we may fairly rank our author in virtue of his preoccupation with things satyric.

By the time of Petronius the word *satyricon,* as we know from its use as the title of his book, had come to mean the same as Latin *opus satyricum,* a piece of writing roughly equivalent to a *satura* but even more embracing in its scope. The *satura* as written by the Romans, who indeed regarded it as their own particular contribution to literature, was a verse composition of which variety of content was the distinguishing feature.

The traditional founder of the genre was Quintus Ennius[10] (239–169 B.C.), a Calabrian whom Cato the Elder brought to Rome, where he earned a living teaching Greek until his talents as an author gained him the patronage of influential men like the Scipios who encouraged him in the writing of poetry and drama.

We have only fragments of his work but they are sufficient to show the essential variety of them, as they include fables, didactic pieces, autobiographical detail, and satire on gluttons, busybodies, slanderers and parasites. We see enough to realize that Horace, who proclaims Ennius the founder of *satura,* carried on his tradition in his own "satires."

Petronius' *Satyricon* has the same miscellaneous quality as *satura* but, as we shall see, introduces even more variety of subject matter, everything in fact which belongs to the field of popular literary humor. The greater freedom of the Menippean form, allowing both prose and verse and permitting continuous episodic narrative, enables the inclusion of representative portions of what are in themselves separate genres from the Greek and Roman heritage.

Satyricon resumes within its elastic frame the sum of the literary and artistic preoccupations of the leisured young men about town of Nero's day with a penchant for the popular in entertainment, a vogue fostered by the emperor himself to win and retain the affection of the masses by sharing in their lighter moods.

As the neuter adjective evolved from its basic meaning of "Satyr-like" to encompass the activities of the Roman scions of Faunus, so too the masculine *satyricos* evolved in its company and acquired the significance of a devotee of the theater arts, a habitué of the Palaestra.[11] This latter, the school of dramatic art of the Greco-Roman world, had for its legendary founder and patron the god Hermes, the Roman Mercury, so that men of culture are sometimes called *Mercuriales.* The link with Romanized satyric tradition is shown by Horace's tribute to Faunus as the guardian of the men of Mercury (*Faunus, Mercurialium custos virorum—Odes,* 2.17.28).

Like the stage-door johnnies of a later age, the young ne'er-do-wells of imperial Rome who neglected the responsibilities of their social status in order to enjoy the allurements of song and dance, music and merriment and who, like Terence's Phaedria, escorted the girls to and from their guitar practice, got themselves a bad name. Their devotion to the satyric arts confirmed the lascivious connotation which *satyricos* by its very derivation implied. There can be no doubt whatever that they rejoiced in this devil-may-care reputation.

The precise meaning of *satyricos* in Nero's world and its close association with the theater and Palaestra is well brought out in a passage from Plutarch's *Life of Galba,* Chapter 16.

Galba, Nero's successor, was determined to economize, especially in the matter of throwing public money about on entertainment. And so, Plutarch says, he ordered that the gifts which had been made to people of the theater and *palaestra* should be handed back, all but a tenth part. In this he was disappointed, for most of the beneficiaries had squandered the money, being men who lived only for the day (*ephemeroi*) and satyric (*satyricoi*) in their way of life. The word *satyricoi* is here meant to convey loose and feckless conduct, but is specifically applied to the adherents of the theater world (*hoi peri skenen kai palaistran* runs the Greek).

People who live for the day and whose behavior is marked by laxity and irresponsibility—Plutarch's remark admirably sums up a kind of temperament commonly found among theatrical folk and those attracted to their world, a world affected by the young bloods of Petronius' and his master's entourage. They are *satyricoi* and so is their guide and instructor in the arts of luxurious and refined living. Nero called Petronius his *Arbiter elegantiarum.* The fourth-century grammarian Marius Victorinus[12] calls him *Arbiter Satyricon* (here genitive plural)—"the Arbiter of things satyric." Thus *satyrica* are the current vogue and constitute the media through which refinement (*elegantiae*) is sought. The *satyricoi* are the practitioners of these arts of refinement and Petronius is, as it were, the chief *Satyricos* among them.

Through the emperor, in one sense the divine descendant of Faunus, a father of the Roman people, special sanction is given to the Fauni, the Latin cousins of the Satyrs. The antics of their votaries are centered about the stage and *palaestra,* those mirrors of life, and find official approval as confirming the divine origin of the Roman popular heritage of humor. Not only Faunus, but also Apollo and Mercury are duly honored. Mercury in particular, as we shall see, is the patron of the activities depicted in the *Satyricon,* not least as the protector of the wandering students who are its protagonists. It is he who finally delivers them from the wrathful wiles of Priapus, a triumph for Rome over the noisome cult of a foreign superstition, the like of which Suetonius tells us Nero abhorred (Suetonius, *Nero,* 56).

V *The Ingredients of* Satyricon

We have seen that Petronius' *Satyricon,* a unique work in literature, is a burlesque of humanity, cast in the form of Menippean satire and an embodiment of the Roman satyric tradition. A long episodic narrative, conceived as a court entertainment in response to a prevailing vogue inspired by Nero's sympathy for the theater arts in their more popular aspects, it is held together by a continuous thread—the adventures of a young student, a *scholasticus,* to employ Petronius' term, called Encolpius and his boy lover Giton. In the first part of the work he has for his constant companion another student, Ascyltos, and in the second part an older man, a beggar poet and philosopher, Eumolpus. These wandering scholars, the spiritual ancestors of those whose antics plagued the medieval church, but who also penned some of the loveliest lyrics and the most delicious satire in all Latin literature,[13] meet up with all sorts of people from the less edifying strata of mankind and their combined activities provide a fascinating picture of life in the Greco-Latin world of the mid-first century.

We shall expect to find in the *Satyricon* the various elements which constitute *satyrica,* that is to say elements derived from the literary genres of the popular humorous tradition—satyric drama, mime,[14] satura, folklore, and romance.

Needless to say, these elements overlap and intermingle in the course of the narrative, but all are discernible. Unfortunately, our knowledge of satyric drama and of mime is so fragmentary that we cannot pinpoint their separate influences, although certain of the situations in the *Satyricon* are redolent of the kind of thing we know to have furnished the plot and characterization of one or the other of these popular entertainments.

These elements will be referred to in the analysis of the *Satyricon* in Chapter 3. It will suffice here to give a brief outline of the genres they represent.

A. Satyric drama.

Upon Italian soil the dramatic forms which are acknowledged to derive from the Greek satyr play no longer provide light relief to follow a triple dose of tragedy, as at the fifth-century Dionysia of Athens. Even the characteristic chorus of goat-skin clad clowns is lost. This is because goatishness has taken over the whole concept of the Italian derivatives, invading the action itself and imparting to it a strong flavor of farce and obscenity.

It is true that Roman grammarians speak of the *genus satyricum* as something midway between tragedy and comedy. By this they mean that it parodies the themes of tragedy, treating them as comedy. The nearest thing we possess to fit this definition is Plautus' *Amphitruo,* a burlesque of Jupiter's legendary amorous pursuit of Alcumena, wife of Amphitruo, king of Thebes, which Plautus himself described as a tragi-comedy (*Amphitruo,* 50–59).

But this particular form of satyric drama does not seem to have caught on at Rome. Instead, the satyric tradition came to be identified with a genre apparently native to Italy, the Atellan farce, and Diomedes, no doubt quoting Varro, refers to *fabula Atellana* as the Latin equivalent of the Greek *fabula Satyrica.*[15] This farce originated in the Greek communities of Southern Italy (Magna Graecia) and was developed in particular at Atella in Campania. Its early form seems to have been improvised farce centered about stock characters whose names have been recorded—Maccus the Clown, Pappus the Old Dotard, Bucco the Boaster, Dossennus the Hunchback.

But by the time of Sulla the Dictator, 138–78 B.C., a more definite literary form had been given to the Atellan play by Pomponius Bononiensis (ca. 100–85) and Novius (ca. 95–80). These two preserved the parody of mythological and legendary themes of the Greek satyr plays and the vulgarity and knock-about farce of the original satyr choruses. A special meter, no doubt of Greek origin, was employed in these plays, significantly called the satyric or priapeic meter of which the grammarians give examples.[16] It was a hexameter, achieving lightness and speed by the frequent use of trisyllabic feet, the dactyl, the anapest, and especially the tribrach, in addition to the spondee normal to the hexameter and the iambus and trochee characteristic of popular verse and in particular the jesting, carping *satura* poem. The native Italian Saturnian meter was also employed in Atellan farce, a verse which, the early grammarians tell us, consisted of two clearly defined halves and which, in metrical terms, may be described as three iambi plus a half-foot (to mark the pause), followed by three trochees.[17] This latter half bears the significant title of ithyphallic (erect phallus), clearly establishing its connection with primitive satyric fertility ritual.

B. Mime.

Closely linked with Atellan plays in popular esteem and enjoying a great vogue in Nero's time was the farcical and indecent mime. The mimetic instinct is strong in primitive peoples and from early times solo performers or small companies in Greece and doubtless also in Italy, whether under Greek influence or independently, gave imitations of the voice and gestures of men and animals and presented short scenes from daily life, sometimes in prose, sometimes in verse, with or without musical accompaniment.

A notable feature of mime is the representation of women in farcical, lascivious, and disreputable situations, women acrobats, dancers, concubines, quack doctors, sorceresses, and poisoners, adventuresses, stepmothers, jealous mistresses, and participants in erotic festivals.

At Rome, naked women mime performers (*mimae*) were a regular feature of the Floralia, a festival in honor of the fertility goddess Flora. Sulla, himself a writer of *satyrica*, also patronized mime, as did Julius Caesar who ordered a competition between two leading composers of the genre, Decimus Laberius and Publilius Syrus. The latter was highly thought of in Nero's day, commended by Seneca and quoted by Petronius.

There must have been a marked similarity between the everyday scenes of low life mimicked in these performances and the farcical plots of the Atellan play. Many of the situations involving shady characters in our author's work are reminiscent of one or the other genre. The richly comic interlude in Chapters 12 to 15 where Encolpius and Ascyltos try to sell in the marketplace the cloak they have stolen is an example. The parody of popular superstition and absurd ritual in the chapters immediately following (16–26) is another. A third is the farcical adventure of Encolpius, Giton, and Eumolpus in the land of the legacy hunters (chaps. 116 onwards). Indeed, Petronius may have borrowed ideas for this episode from a mime mentioned by Cicero—"The Beggar turned Millionaire" (*Philippics,* 2.65).

C. Satura.

We have mentioned this category in Section III above (p. 33), noting that this characteristically Roman product is bound up with satyric tradition. Roman satyr figures are loquacious as well as lascivious; their goatlike aggressiveness is associated with the mordant satirical spirit of the Italian genius. That the Romans could employ the Menippean variety of *satura* with the same devastating effect as other forms of the genre is shown in the Claudius satire attributed to Seneca; the novelty of Petronius' use of Menippean lies largely in the generous spirit shown therein. The humor is kindly and tolerant, not cruel and condemning.

Our author makes much use of the conventional themes of *satura* which, in this respect like comedy and mime, is concerned with everyday existence. But there is an important difference between the preoccupations of literary *satura* and those of comedy and mime. *Satura* strikes a more intellectual note. Its essential character as a medley makes it an admirable vehicle for the critique of ideas, an interchange of opinions and comment upon philosophy, literature, social and even, when the temper of the times permits, political problems and personalities.

The satires of Lucilius and Horace were called *sermones,* that is conversations, and they owe something to the "street sermons" of Hellenistic times, delivered by philosophers upon ethical problems, made palatable by humorous treatment in colloquial language, spiced with jokes and epigrams, parodies of poetry and of rhetoric.

This kind of conversation among educated men is ideally carried on over a meal. And so the banquet (*symposium*) is a traditional *mise-en-scène* in *satura*, perhaps with a hint of the notion of repletion inherent in the word *satur,* where the flow of ideas is stimulated by food and drink and a relaxed mood admits of a merry treatment of serious topics.

In Petronius we find the banquet convention exploited to the full in Trimalchio's dinner party which occupies about one third of the extant fragments of the *Satyricon* and there are other, more modest meals (e.g. chaps. 16, 92, and 109) to mark the tradition.

Discussions of philosophy, art, literature, and rhetoric abound in the work (e.g. chaps. 1–5, 83–90, 118) and the frequent incursions into verse according with the Menippean genre permit the illustration of ideas and methods of composition. The two topical themes of the day for poetry, the Taking of Troy (Nero's favorite) and the Civil War (the subject of Lucan's epic) run to 65 and 295 lines respectively.

D. Romance.

The *Satyricon* is formally cast in the mould of Menippean satire and much of its contents conforms to the traditional themes of *satura.* But the narrative structure of the work achieves a continuity which is lacking in Roman satirical poetry and here Petronius' debt is to the novel of love and adventure, romantic in flavor and rhetorical in exposition, of which Greek literature gives us five complete examples as well as some fragments.[18] These examples are all of later date than our *Satyricon,* but the genre must have existed in Greek as in Oriental literatures from the earliest times.

These romantic novels are a literary development of the oral tradition of the wandering storyteller, a humbler counterpart of the heroic bard. Indeed, earlier fragments of these romances suggest that myth and legend supplied the subject matter for them as for the epic poems of a Homer, while popular heroes like Alexander the Great were the inspiration for a whole cycle of fantastic accounts which were perpetuated into the Middle Ages.

Side by side with these semi-historical compilations were stories of the doings of purely fictional characters. Typical of the latter are the vicissitudes of young lovers as described by Chariton (second century A.D.), Achilles Tatius and Longus (third century A.D.). The course of true love is interrupted by misfortunes and dangers of the direst, including such things as capture, enslavement, shipwreck, unwelcome suitors, and other trials of virtue and loyalty.

There can be no doubt that Petronius had in mind this kind of thing in composing his narrative, but, in obedience to the satyric tradition, he treats his material in serio-comic vein. The trials of the homosexual lovers Encolpius and Giton, the strife caused by the invasion of their intimacy first by Ascyltos and then by Eumolpus are a parody of those encountered by the boys and girls of the Greek romances like Longus' Daphnis and Chloe, Tatius' Leucippe and Clitophon. At regular intervals in the *Satyricon* we have lovers' quarrels, as in chaps. 6–11, 79–82 and 91–99. The sea voyage and shipwreck (chaps. 100–124) are part of the convention too, as also the occasional intervention of benignant or invidious deities like Mercury, Fortuna, and Priapus. On the other hand, the travesty of the wanderings of Odysseus in the wanderings of Encolpius, which actually include an encounter with a Circe (chaps. 126–131), is in the direct tradition of satyr drama.

E. Folklore.

This category, although scarcely a literary genre, is necessarily inherent in the satyric tradition since the latter embraces all that pertains to popular entertainment, except of course the purely physical attractions of athletic contests, racing, gladiatorial combats, and so on.

A notable feature of the *Satyricon* is the satirical treatment of popular superstitions and religious cults, especially that of Priapus. The ridicule to which the women votaries of the god are subjected owes something we may be sure to the prevailing popularity of mime, but the vagaries of superstitious practice are part and parcel of folklore and must have provided the itinerant *raconteurs* of the Roman world, the *circulatores* to whom Petronius refers in Chapter 68, with much juicy material. The absurd propitiatory rites with their obscene details described in Chapters 19–26 and again in 135–138 are typical of the sort of thing with which they regaled their street audiences.

Two striking examples of the folk tale are provided within the framework of Trimalchio's dinner party. They are the werewolf story told by Niceros in Chapters 61–62 and Trimalchio's own experience with witches related in 73.

Another folklore element which Petronius employs is the Milesian tale, named after Aristides of Miletus (ca. 100 B.C.), who wrote a collection of them called *Milesiaca*. Ovid and Plutarch refer to them as erotic and obscene. They enjoyed great popularity at Rome, thanks to a translation made of them by the historian Cornelius Sisenna, the opponent of Cicero in the prosecution of Verres in 70 B.C. Petronius makes use of two magnificent examples of the genre, the Pergamene Boy (chaps. 85–87) and the Matron of Ephesus (chaps. 101–102), both related by Eumolpus.

VI *The Categorical Arrangement of the* Satyricon

A critical examination of the *Satyricon* as we now possess it would seem to indicate that the work was not ruthlessly and indiscriminately mutilated by outraged ecclesiastics and monastic scribes into the fragments which have come down to us. Had this been the case, one feels that they would indeed have deprived us of much that remains.

Petronius' book must have been of considerable length, but not I think anything like so vast as has been supposed. The notion that our present fragments represent only the fifteenth and sixteenth books of the whole work derives from the Trau manuscript (of late date—1423) and from a letter by the Italian humanist Poggio who, also in 1423, wrote to a friend that he had procured from Cologne a manuscript of the fifteenth book of Petronius. The information given in the Trau manuscript in all probability derives from the Cologne manuscript (now lost), or from its immediate source. To my mind the figures given must be the result of an error of transcription. Even if there were in all no more than sixteen books this would mean that the original work was enormous, far too large for its obvious purpose as a court entertainment. One cannot imagine Nero sitting through such a recital. Furthermore, it is difficult to see why only the final part of the work should have been preserved.

It is far more reasonable to suppose that the original *Satyricon*, like other meritorious works of considerable length, was systematically abridged by an *epitomator*, probably in the fourth or fifth century. I use the word systematically because an analysis of our extant fragments in terms of the literary genres mentioned above indicates an intention to preserve a representative choice of such genres, with some evidence of method in arrangement of them. I have drawn up a tentative plan following the order of the chapters so as to illustrate this contention. Our fragments seem to arrange themselves in twelve sections, labeled by reference to one or more genres contained therein:

1. SATURA—chaps. 1–5—a discussion of contemporary oratory followed by illustrative verse.
2. ROMANCE—chaps. 6–11—parody of lovers' adventures and quarrels.
3. MIME/ATELLANA—chaps. 12–15—the farcical scenes of the attempt to sell a stolen cloak.
4. ROMANCE + FOLKLORE + MIME/ATELLANA—chaps. 16–26—the incidents following the alleged profanation of Priapic

rites, with parody of popular superstitions, Oriental cults, and propitiation ceremonies.

5. SATURA + FOLKLORE—chaps. 26–78—the dinner party and the various anecdotes inserted.
6. ROMANCE—chaps. 79–82—continuation of the lovers' vicissitudes.
7. SATURA + FOLKLORE—chaps. 83–90—discussion of art and morals followed by illustrative verse (The Capture of Troy). A Milesian Tale is inserted (The Pergamene Boy).
8. ROMANCE—chaps. 91–99—continuation of the lovers' vicissitudes.
9. ROMANCE + FOLKLORE—chaps. 100–115—The Sea Voyage, a conventional framework for romance, like the dinner party for *satura,* with elements of folklore, mythology, and possibly mime.
10. MIME/ATELLANA—chaps. 116–117—the plan for deceiving the fortune hunters of Croton is obviously in this tradition.
11. SATURA—chaps. 118–124—discussion on poetry followed by illustrative verse (The Civil War).
12. ROMANCE + FOLKLORE + MIME—chaps. 125–141—the adventures at Croton, the affair with Circe and her servants, with parody of superstitious rites.

The grotesque provisions of Eumolpus' testament are obvious mime material.

The plan outlined above shows a fairly even distribution of the various elements, which are skillfully blended to give homogeneity to the whole work. It seems clear that the epitomist has done his job well in preserving selections truly representative of the original whole while reducing it to a scope amenable to the reader and possibly removing scenes considered unnecessarily obscene or perhaps superfluous and repetitive.

A certain balance is also discernible. The two main conventional cadres, the banquet and the ship, are placed at equal intervals respectively from the beginning and end of the epitome, although it may be a coincidence that exactly twenty-six chapters occur before the beginning of the banquet episode (1–26) and exactly twenty-six from the end of the ship episode to the end of our fragments (115–141). The interval between the end of the banquet and the beginning of the ship episode is also roughly the same length—twenty-one chapters (79–100).

Thus there are roughly five divisions of the work—1. before the banquet, 2. the banquet, 3. between banquet and ship, 4. ship, 5. after the ship.

Continuity in the narrative is maintained by the fact that Encolpius is the narrator throughout and everything which occurs concerns him in some way, either directly or as a source of reflection and comment. Over and above this, purely from the structural point of view in terms of the categories mentioned in the plan above, the sections are held together by the framework of the lovers' adventures, that is sections 2, 4, 6, 8, and 12 which are primarily and ipso facto of the category "romance."

Another structural support is provided by the three *satura* sections of literary, philosophic, or artistic discussion—sections 1, 7, and 11.

The two main beams of the structure are the banquet (*satura*) and ship (romance) episodes, placed, as we have seen, at roughly equidistant intervals. The disparity in their respective lengths is no doubt to be accounted for by the greater proportion of lacunae in the ship episode which originally may have pretty well equaled the banquet's fifty odd chapters.

CHAPTER 3

The Satyricon *Analyzed*[1]

THE work as we have it is fragmentary, but the fragments are for the most part large and there is a considerable amount of linkage. It is divided into 141 chapters. Both the beginning of Chapter 1 and the end of Chapter 141 are missing. The action takes place, 1. in a Greco-Latin community of Campania, unnamed but referred to as a "Greek city," 2. on board a ship bound for Tarentum, 3. at Croton on the toe of Italy.

I *Chapters 1–5. Encolpius on Oratory. Agamemnon replies*

The opening scene is the portico of a school of rhetoric in the *Graeca urbs*, the setting of our heroes' adventures until the end of Chapter 99, a seaside town in Campania, in all probability Puteoli on the Bay of Naples.

We do not know why they are here, whether driven by the hazard of their wandering condition or attracted by the reputation of the head of the school, Agamemnon. He seems hardly the type to command much authority and keeps pretty low company on occasion. The vulgar Trimalchio treats him with little respect when he invites him and some of his students to his extravagant table.

Encolpius, a young pupil of Agamemnon, narrator of the *Satyricon* and leading spirit of the trio whose escapades are the main theme of the book, is holding forth in an eloquent tirade against the so-called Asiatic school of rhetorical practice, with its extravagantly unreal subjects for debate: tyrants ordering sons to murder their fathers, pirates pleading their cause in chains, prophetic utterances to avert a plague with the sacrifice of maidens.

These outrageous themes are pleaded in language just as outrageous, with exaggeration, bombast, and honeyed words. Such hollow-sounding verbiage and ridiculous word play rob eloquence of its vitality. Not only oratory, but poetry and painting too have been debased by Oriental influence, says Encolpius.

Agamemnon agrees and praises the young man's common sense. But what else can we do? If we teachers of rhetoric do not whet the appetites of our hearers with such extravagance, then we shall find our classrooms empty. The parents are to blame; they are too anxious for their sons to get rich quick as orators and do not give their minds time to mellow with protracted study of the best models.

The scene is not prolonged, for Petronius never bores us and the subject of rhetoric is tedious. But he makes his point. There is too much Asiatic and Hellenistic oratory about, pervading with its claptrap and excessive ornamentation the native talent of sturdy Rome. Parents concerned for their children's education should avoid submitting them to these bad influences. Let reason prevail. Petronius takes a brief opportunity to expound his own conviction.

In accordance with *satura* tradition this discussion is pointed by an outburst of verse, exhorting the would-be practitioner of a noble art to steep himself in the masters, Demosthenes and Cicero.

II *Chapters 6–11. Escape into Embarrassment*

We are presented in Chapter 6 with the amusing picture of a crowd of *scholastici* leaving the classroom after a declamation, making fun of the arguments and the presentation of the speech by one of the pupils. They crowd into the portico, and Encolpius, who has suddenly noticed that his friend Ascyltos is missing, is able to slip away unnoticed and go after him. But he loses his way, being unfamiliar with the town. And so we learn that our wandering students are strangers in this Greek city.

At last, worn out with fruitless searching, he accosts an old woman selling country produce. "Tell me, Mother," he says, "you don't happen to know where I live?" "Of course I do," she replies and proceeds to guide him. This remark of Encolpius reveals the joker in him; he has the satyric spirit. He is the city wit, a type characteristic in Latin literature and to whom the Romans give the name *scurra*. He develops into the clown of medieval times and is to be found in the ranks of their wandering scholars, retaining his Latin name.

The old woman is also a practical joker and has conducted our hero into a brothel, remarking "This must be where you live." Encolpius is about to flee from perdition when, lo and behold, Ascyltos runs to meet him, for a respectable householder (*pater familias*, ironically) has guided him there too. The *pater familias* brothel keeper is a delightful piece of satyric fun.

The two students arrive back at their lodging house to find Giton, a sixteen-year-old boy who is Encolpius' lover, waiting for them on the pavement outside. He tearfully explains to Encolpius that Ascyltos has been trying to force his attentions upon him. The two friends roundly abuse each other until the humor of the situation makes them come to terms. They burst out laughing at Ascyltos' remark that Encolpius is the baser scoundrel of the two since he actually praised a poet to secure an invitation to dine. Such jibing at poets as the greatest of all evils is a commonplace of first-century humor.

But the two decide to part company, as Encolpius is still smarting from the other's treachery. Tomorrow they will go their separate ways. Tonight they are invited to a dinner as *scholastici*—a sidelight on contemporary practice. Men of letters can get a free meal because they can grace a table with cultured conversation. This incidentally is precisely what Encolpius and his companions do not do on this particular occasion.

III *Chapters 12–15. Mime in the Market*

Wandering scholars are under the twofold protection of Mercury, the patron of the *palaestra* and also of travelers. On occasion they are not above a little pilfering to swell their meager funds. Here too the indulgent god takes them under his wing, for he is not least the helper of those who help themselves.

Our heroes have purloined a cloak which they now offer for sale in the marketplace as twilight descends, this being the best time to dispose of second-hand goods whose defects are blurred by the obscurity. A country yokel steps up to examine the garment and to their amazement, the friends notice that he is wearing a cloak belonging to Encolpius, which he had left behind somewhere. Luckily, the thief has not noticed that some gold pieces had been sewn up in the lining. Encolpius is for having recourse to the law, but Ascyltos restrains him. No one will support our claim, for we are strangers to this place! He advises that they purchase back the garment for a small sum, in order to regain their treasure.

The verses which follow (Chapter 14) are singularly reminiscent of the favorite theme of the *Carmina Burana*,[2] the satiric poems of the twelfth-century wandering scholars. Of what use are the laws, where money alone is king? Poverty has no rights, the magistrates are corrupt (*Carmina Burana*, 1.11).

A quarrel breaks out. Some night-bound lawyers intervene, scenting litigation. To settle the business quickly, the cloaks are exchanged, each party content with this arrangement.

The whole episode is pure farce, an admirable plot for mime or Atellan play with stock characters, the dim-witted rustic, the needy scholar, the pettifogging lawyer. Petronius treats us to a slice of low life with the utmost realism of detail.

IV *Chapters 16–26. The Priestess of Priapism*

The trio have just finished their supper, prepared by Giton, and are congratulating themselves on the recovery of their precious garment, when the door of their lodging is subjected to such a pounding that the lock is shattered and falls to the ground. A woman appears who announces herself as the servant of one Quartilla. The students have somehow violated a sacred ritual in honor of Priapus which was being conducted near the entrance to the Crypta Neapolitana, an underground passage running between Puteoli and Naples. Quartilla demands an audience with the offenders. She is not really angry with them but rather curious to find out what god has brought such attractive young men to her part of the world.

There now follows a delightful satire on the cult of Priapus and its feminine adherents and no doubt, by implication, on other Eastern fertility cults, so popular in the Roman world of the first century. We have a superb bit of acting from Quartilla who obviously lives her part with conviction—a true tragedy queen. She sits there on Encolpius' bed, weeping copiously, and wringing her hands until the joints crack. She professes pity for the malefactors, whose punishment is certain. It is a dangerous quarter for the innocent abroad; there are so many divinities in the area that they are more common than mortals. Thus Petronius tilts at the all-pervading nature of these noxious religions among the lower quarters of a region of Italy largely occupied by people of foreign extraction.

The poor woman has had a sleepless night thinking of their sad case, but she is chiefly concerned that the mysteries of Priapus shall not be divulged, thus turning to ridicule an age-old ritual known scarcely to a thousand persons in all!

Quartilla is the first important woman character in the book, the first of many vivid, amusing, and entirely human feminine portraits. They make a pleasing contrast with their contemporaries in high society of whom the pages of Tacitus are full and who are either paragons of outraged virtue, genuinely piteous victims of brutality, or mistresses of iniquity.

We gather from these introductory chapters preceding the Banquet of Trimalchio (Chapters 1–26) that Petronius has considerable contempt for these popular Eastern practices. They were apparently monopolized by women, took place at night, and included wild orgies of a sexual nature which the ladies contrived to perform without masculine help.

Rome was no stranger to such goings-on. As early as 186 B.C., the Senate had been compelled to pass a decree forbidding such feminine riots in honor of Bacchus, god of wine and also of fertility in general, whose devotees were prone to excesses hardly in keeping with the dignity of Roman matrons. Plautus in his *Amphitruo* makes reference to these rites by suggesting that Alcumena has become mad like a Bacchanal (*Amphitruo*, 702–705). Evidently, the matrons did not need much persuading to adopt new rites to supplant the forbidden Bacchanalia.

Petronius' treatment of his women characters shows his usual tolerant humor, but he does not show them in too favorable a light for all that. The absence of any really edifying female portrait in his work perhaps indicates that he is something of a misogynist. I would suggest that he was probably unmarried and this may be the explanation. There is something of the spirit of the medieval jest books in his attitude to women, and there may be an echo of sentiments shared by wandering scholars who avoid any permanent tie with the fair sex.

The scenes described in these chapters are sticky with crude debauchery. The ludicrous handling of them is so much more effective than the grim seriousness of a nagging Tacitus, a vice-obsessed Suetonius, or a Juvenal beside himself with savage indignation. It is certainly true that there is no evidence of conscious moral purpose in the *Satyricon.* We do not expect it from the chosen companion of Nero. The Arbiter is not a satirist in the usually accepted sense, either seriously like Juvenal, playfully like Horace, or with tongue in cheek like Martial. He is not trying to reform the world or to vent his disgust or personal animosity, nor is he cloaking a love of obscenity under the pretext of chastising the vices of an age.

In a sense he is above all this, for he does not depend upon a patron for a living. Certainly he is trying to please an audience, but we feel that he is an independent spirit, that perhaps the audience chose him as much as he chose it. His work is unique and something entirely new, its keynote one of escape, reflected in the wanderings of its main characters.

Not only is there no moral purpose in the *Satyricon;* there is perhaps not even a message for its hearers, the court circle. But there is one for us, its readers in the light of history. Its author and others like him in his day were not at ease in their lives. Their extravagances and debaucheries were an escape from a perilous and unstable society of which they sensed the inevitable decline and decay.

The most striking features of Petronius' work are precisely its good humor and tolerance. They strike a false note in an age of extreme cruelty and oppression. They are completely unreal and their unreality is the mark of the author's escapism. Nero too was an escapist, but he took refuge into a mad world, that of an emperor turned actor and charioteer. Petronius was sane and his escape is into the world of ordinary men and women, a world, be it noted, remote from that in which he had his being.

Here then is the astonishing thing about the *Satyricon*—the vices it portrays are unreal in that they fall far short of the vices of the milieu in which it was composed. The conduct of Encolpius and his companions is innocence itself compared to that of Petronius' circle. Was not his audience in some way conscious of this understatement of the truth? If so, did they not feel an uneasiness when thus confronted with a kind of inverted satire of themselves? Did the Arbiter overreach himself and drive the emperor the more surely into the clutches of Tigellinus?

V *The Banquet Episode*

The banquet is a literary convention in classical literature. It provides a natural setting for conversation and the discussion of philosophy, literature, art, and life in general. The opportunity for protracted convivial entertainment among cultured citizens was greater in the ancient world than it is now, because of the leisure and facility provided by slave labor. It is a curious paradox that the intellectual achievement of antiquity was so largely permitted by an inhuman and degrading institution, whereby the incessant and unrewarded effort of the majority of a population provided freedom for the happy few to produce those masterpieces of thought and artistic creation which we admire today and which have so much influenced the centuries in between. The *Symposia* of Plato and Xenophon set a partly serious, partly jesting pattern which was ideal for expressing truths in palatable form. A literary genre was evolved which provided an excellent vehicle for the satirist.

Petronius bows to convention in inserting a banquet as part of the *Satyricon,* where it constituted a Menippean satire within a Menippean satire. The *Cena Trimalchionis* (Trimalchio's Dinner Party) is a self-contained unit with, as it were, an independent existence, which is why the epitomator preserved it more or less whole, as it is not too long and the reverse of tedious to read.

At the same time, the episode has been linked with the earlier and later incidents, for Encolpius is still the narrator and he and his fellow students are among the guests together with their teacher Agamemnon, through whom in fact the invitation has been secured. The curious thing is that, although the *scholastici* have been in theory invited to contribute cultural tone, none of them is apparently allowed to make such a contribution. Trimalchio considers himself perfectly capable of supplying any cultural offerings needed. Both he and his other guests are inclined to slight the students and their teacher.

Petronius is highly satirical in this episode, but not unsympathetic towards Trimalchio and his fellow freedmen. He clearly shows that they are incapable of the higher reaches of intellectual conversation (the true purpose of the banquet genre), but they are able to provide entertainment for themselves which is rich in popular humor and practical insight into human foibles. There is much shrewd criticism of the defects of contemporary society and its politics.

The *Cena* is fast-moving narrative with interest sustained by surprise and comic detail. It is also a series of vivid portraits of the freedman class of Greek and Eastern origin, whose colloquial Latinity is reproduced by the author with obvious exactitude. This aspect makes the episode one of the most valuable documents we possess for the study of living Latin, the speech whose grammatical and syntactical forms are the basis from which developed the modern Romance languages.

VI *Chapters 26–30. The Rally of Refinement*

The epitomator (or was it some church father a century or so later?) decided we could do without the rest of the lecherous details of Quartilla's expiation ceremonies. She and her crew of celebrants disappear like witches banished by the stroke of a purist pen.

After the ensuing gap in the text our friends are discovered lying exhausted on their beds, where they are allowed to pass the rest of the night in peace. Next morning a servant of Agamemnon arrives to remind them of what appears to them in their weary and demoralized condition to be yet another ordeal. However, it may at least be sustaining. Today they are to eat at the house of one Trimalchio, a most refined gent (*lautissimus homo*) whose time is so valuable that he keeps a clock in his dining room (the very last place a Roman would wish to be reminded) and a bugler in uniform to announce the fleeting hours.

The guests hasten to a private bathhouse, and at once the note of extravagance is sounded which will echo through the whole episode. Trimalchio the host is a bald old man dressed in a russet mantle and playing ball with long-haired Alexandrian slave boys, chosen for their good looks, while a eunuch attendant stands by holding a silver chamber pot in constant readiness. The master does not fail to use it and having done so, sprinkles his fingers with water and wipes them on the convenient locks of one of the ball players.

The details of this scene set the pace for the whole. Everything connected with Trimalchio's appearance and surroundings is colorful, bizarre, and expensive. He affects, besides his russet gown, others of scarlet, green, and cerise. His attendants are similarly arrayed. Petronius stresses the host's love of bright colors as well as of noise. He must have music wherever he goes. These things are held by the Arbiter to be discordant with the true refinement which is his métier. We are to be treated to a satire on bad taste.

Trimalchio leaves the bathhouse to dress for the feast. He is accompanied by a musician who plays into his ear, as though whispering secrets, a gentle music from tiny Pan pipes. At the entrance to the house stands a doorkeeper resplendent in green and cherry, shelling peas into a silver bowl. Above his head is a golden cage with a magpie to greet the guests.

Close by the doorkeeper's cell is a painting of a huge mastiff with the inscription "Beware of the Dog." It frightens the guests and shocks them into noticing the mural decorations of the entrance hall. They depict, as one would guess, the master's career. Trimalchio, arriving from his Asiatic place of origin, is a long-haired slave boy like the companions of his ball practice. He is shown entering Puteoli with Mercury as his guide to ensure his future as a businessman. The details are given of his triumphant career, starting as a bookkeeper and ending on the magistrate's bench.

The introduction of Mercury at this point is significant. He links Trimalchio with Encolpius and his fellow students, being patron of them all, as god of businessmen, scholars, and travelers. He is the presiding deity of the whole work and is finally triumphant on behalf of all his protégés against Priapus, Fortuna, Isis, Hercules, Neptune, and whatever others may have intervened in the course of the original narrative to upset the lives of its protagonists.

Fortuna is present in the picture gallery with her horn of plenty and also the three Fates, weaving the gold threads of Trimalchio's life. We are reminded of the similar scene in the Claudius satire attributed to Seneca, where the gold threads are those of Nero's life. But we cannot suppose that our author would have dared to make a deliberate comparison between the emperor and the vulgar freedman who is Trimalchio. Rather must we conclude that the image was a commonplace, not likely to arouse suspicion.

We now learn from a piece of pretentious heraldry that our host's names are Gaius Pompeius Trimalchio. This means that his late master, from whom he obtained his freedom, was called Pompeius. The latter name, as mentioned above, is deliberately chosen to fit the Campanian setting. We learn in Chapter 71 that Trimalchio also has a fourth name, Maecenatianus, implying that before being sold to Pompeius, he belonged to a Maecenas. The fact that the Pompeii, like the Maecenates and the Petronii, owned estates in Egypt as well as in Campania strongly suggests that the Arbiter has based his portrait of Trimalchio upon an actual acquaintance.

Another piece of vulgar display is a tablet affixed to the door post showing a plan of the moon and the seven planets in their course, so that the days lucky and unlucky for business ventures may be duly calculated. Belief in astrology, so prevalent at the time, was for Petronius a mark of bad taste. Furthermore, it is necessary to cross the threshold of the dining room right foot first, a piece of superstition which Trimalchio, for all his affluence, has not learned to dispense with.

VII *Chapters 31–36. Novelty upon Novelty in Dazzling Display*

Each successive detail of the evolving setting for the feast calls forth admiration which is tempered by astonishment. It is made obvious to us that the proceedings are far from customary. Trimalchio displays great ingenuity in devising new means of entertainment. In this he is doing his utmost to comply with the current craze for novelty, the only possible antidote to the malady of the times—boredom. The upper strata of society in which Petronius moves suffer from the same complaint. Trimalchio is only doing what Petronius himself has to do to please the court—surprise them into amusement, his only fault being that he goes about it the wrong way. In Chapter 31 the guests receive foot treatment from a team of pedicurists who actually sing while engaged upon their unpleasant task. All the servants of Trimalchio's household have in fact been trained to sing or play musical instruments while performing their duties. Such conduct is reminiscent of the schools of theater arts, and we are made to feel that Trimalchio is himself a *satyricos,* which means that he has the right ideas, if only he knew how to interpret them with taste and discernment. Encolpius remarks that the attendants of the dining room remind him of a chorus of pantomime. It is not pantomime itself which is criticized but the misuse of it.

Not least among the novelties of the occasion is the belated but carefully timed entrance of the host. He makes his appearance when the guests have already been regaled with a really choice hors d'oeuvre, the highlight of which are roasted dormice with sauce made from honey spiced with poppy seed. He is conveyed upon a litter and of course accompanied by a band. Extravagantly dressed, he wears a ring which is an imitation of the one worn by Roman knights as a mark of their status and made of solid gold. Trimalchio's is gold-plated and sufficient to suggest no doubt the rank to which his talents should have elevated him. In order not to delay proceedings he had interrupted a game of dice, which he now resumes in front of his guests. They are thus able to note that, instead of ordinary black and white counters, their elegant host plays with gold and silver pieces.

More delicacies are served, including peahens' eggs and stuffed fig-peckers enclosed in shells of pastry. Then the hors d'oeuvres are cleared away by a chorus of slaves singing to music, while wine is provided instead of water for the guests to wash their hands. Each successive feature of this recherché entertainment is greeted by exclamations of delight from those invited. The effect is comic as Petronius drives home with deadly insistence his lessons of bad taste. At times we feel he overdoes this, but we must remember that the Romans were not too subtle. Constant repetition of effect does not seem to dull the edge of satire for them.

"I have ordered," says Trimalchio, "a separate table for each of us. In this way the stinking slaves will make less of a sweat for us with their comings and goings."

The wine is Falernian, put down in the year of Opimius' consulship. If this is genuine, it is older than the hundred years claimed for it, as Opimius was consul in 121 B.C. In his ignorance Trimalchio falls short of the effect he desires to make and in any case of course wine as old as this was probably undrinkable.

The astrological display of dishes which follows the Egyptian movable silver skeleton is apparently something really remarkable and shows the lengths to which the host will go to provide the all-important element of *novitas.* The twelve signs of the zodiac are arranged in a circle on a tray and upon each sign an appropriate article of food is placed. This is a development of the practice of distributing gifts of food to take home after the party. Each item is accompanied by a motto in verse, as in our Christmas crackers. Martial has a book of such mottoes for *apophoreta* ("gifts to take away"). Trimalchio in a dreadful voice renders a chorus from a current mime which presumably contained a scene with *apophoreta.*

More music, while to the rhythmic steps of a ritual dance the upper layer of the tray is removed, revealing capons, sow's udders, and a hare adorned with feathers to represent the legendary winged horse Pegasus. An attendant steps forward to carve the meat. Even he performs to music, with gestures so aggressive that he reminds the guests of a British charioteer fighting to the accompaniment of an organ recital. The fellow's name is Carver. "Carver, carve!" bids the host. Such a *trouvaille* must have required much careful thought.

VIII *Chapters 37–41. The Lady, the Gent, and Genteel Pastimes*

Encolpius is overcome by such brilliance and can eat no more. He is intrigued by the presence of a woman who is hurrying about the place, supervising the arrangements. Oh, that is Fortunata, Trimalchio's wife, his neighbor tells him, and her character is set forth in succinct phrases full of colloquial imagery, one of Petronius' most delightful sketches. She is the apple of her husband's eye. If she tells him it is midnight when it is broad daylight, he will believe her. Shrewd and sober-minded, she can give you good advice but she is a tittle-tattle and malicious and has her likes and dislikes.

But, says the confidant, it is really the master who compels attention. Boundless wealth and land, he does not personally know one in ten of his household staff. He produces everything on his own ground, there isn't a thing you can ask for that he doesn't have. He brought bees from Mount Hymettus to make honey for him and mushroom seed from India. Many of his fellow freedmen are in the same happy situation—oozing with money, like Diogenes there, also a freedman of Pompeius. As for Iulius Proculus, whose father was a freedman, he was once worth a million but lost it through being too trustful. He was an undertaker by profession but lived like a king.

Trimalchio interrupts to give a detailed account of the significance of the astrological fare. Petronius here satirizes a prevailing pastime which for the emperors had a serious purpose. In their uncertainty of the future they lent an anxious ear to the astrologer and, unfortunately for many an influential courtier, to the informer also. A round of applause greets the exposition of the host's ingenuity. Hipparchus and Aratus, leading lights of astrological lore, are nowhere in the picture.

With split-second timing the scene changes to represent a hunt. Suitable cloth covers are spread over the furniture, woven with pictures of huntsmen's nets and beaters armed with spears. Amid terrific uproar, hunting dogs enter the room and run about among the tables. Then follows another tray upon which a huge boar reclines, wearing the *pilleus* or cap of freedom. Tiny suckling pigs, gifts to take home, flank the dish. Another carver appears and, slitting the side of the boar, lets loose a flight of thrushes which are skillfully caught by professional bird catchers with their limed sticks. The point of the incident is presumably to show that Trimalchio has acquired the tastes of a true gentleman by adding hunting to the preoccupations of his new social status.

Encolpius is puzzled as to why the boar is wearing the cap of freedom and makes bold to ask his obliging neighbor. That's easy. Yesterday, this same boar appeared at table. The guests, already replete, dismissed him from service. And so, today, he comes back a free man!

IX *Chapters 42–46. Puteoli and Politics*

Trimalchio now leaves the room in response to nature's summons. The guests breathe a sigh of relief at his departure and fall to conversing freely among themselves for the first time. Up till now their attention has been strained as they watched for the right moment to applaud each stage of the laborious pageant of their entertainment.

Petronius thus conveys their secret detestation of their host whose insufferable conceit and vulgarity they feel compelled to endure. Most of them are wealthy; they do not need the food. Perhaps their former years of servitude and dependence have ingrained the habit of patience. But there is an element of loyalty in their endurance. Trimalchio has shared their past hardships. The richest man among them, he claims their grudging allegiance. Wealth commands admiration, since it provides the pleasures which alone give meaning to life. The Arbiter himself is bound by this same travesty of Epicureanism as understood by the materialistic Roman mind. The artistic temperament can only seek to refine the process of pleasure. The satire of these chapters is not directed at the pursuit of pleasure and sensation but only at the ways in which they are pursued.

Our author's happy device, so wonderfully in keeping with the spirit of the banquet episode, clears the way for a handful of character sketches of unequaled brilliance in the literature of humor. A machine-gun fire of vulgarisms, clichés, proverbs, maxims, and moralizings, a veritable slaughter of grammar and syntax releasing spurts of that vivid imagery which is the very lifeblood of popular speech—this is Petronius' technique of genius. There is nothing like it elsewhere in Latin literature. Only Plautus shares the exuberance, and he is confined by metrical form and the convention of middle-class comedy.

Damas is the first to profit by Trimalchio's temporary exit. Life is short, says he. A day is nothing. Before you can turn round, it's night again. The best thing you can do is to go straight from bed to board. He feels the cold badly, a bath hardly warms him up. A hot drink is the best protection, but wine goes to his head.

Seleucus hasn't much use for baths. Water gradually eats one's substance away. He agrees that a hot drink is best. Anyway, he couldn't bathe today. He has been to a funeral. The man died in spite of a strict diet. It was the doctors who did him in, or perhaps it was just Fate. However, he had a fine funeral, although his wife was sparing of her tears. Women are a lot of vultures.

Seleucus is too gloomy. Phileros points out that Chrysanthus (the dead man) had a good life and rose from nothing to leave a hundred thousand. But he was a tough, quarrelsome fellow. His brother was a better man and generous, who did well in business after a hard start. He was helped by coming into a fortune which he didn't get quite honestly. Let's talk of the living, says Phileros, giving a recital of his deceased acquaintances.

Someone has to get down to realities, and so Ganymedes begins to discuss the cost of living. We learn that it has been a year of drought and famine. Up goes the price of corn, and the magistrates, instead of intervening, are in collusion with the bakers. Such hardship was not uncommon under the Empire, when much potentially productive land was swallowed up in the pleasure parks of country estates. Tacitus (*Annals,* 12, 43, 1–4) tells us of a famine in 51 when an angry mob attacked Claudius in the Forum. It is unlikely that Petronius is referring to any particular occasion, but he may have had in mind the disturbances of 58 at Puteoli (*Annals,* 13, 48, 1) when envoys were sent to Rome to complain of popular unrest at the avarice of the magistrates.

Indeed, Ganymedes complains bitterly of the hardships of the humbler folk, while the big-timers are having a perpetual feast (*semper Saturnalia agunt*). He rambles on about the good old days when the magistrates were conscientious and forthright in dealing with abuses, looking after the corn supply and being friendly to everyone in the street. He puts the present misfortunes down to a lack of religion—no one cares about the gods any more—no troop of virtuous matrons goes barefoot up the hill to the temple of Jupiter to pray for rain. When they did this, the rain came down straightway in bucketfuls and everyone got drenched.

Echion, the second-hand clothes dealer, is not so pessimistic. Puteoli is a pretty good place and it's not the only one in trouble just now. We're far better off than most—it's really a land of roast pig compared to others.

If they can't have bread, they can have circuses. There is to be a show in three days' time. The aedile in charge is Titus, and he sees things big. There are to be gladiators with real steel and no quarter allowed. Titus is so rich that he won't feel at all what he spends on the show, and it will make his name forever. Special items on the program will include three fighting Gauls, a British woman charioteer (Boudicca must have fired the local imagination), and a steward belonging to Glyco who was caught while giving the mistress a good time. Glyco is a fool to give himself away like that. It wasn't the steward's fault. He was only obeying the woman's orders, and she is a no-good anyway.

But Titus has a dangerous rival for votes in Mammaea who intends to give a public banquet. At least he will beat Norbanus (another name borrowed from Petronius' acquaintance among the landowners of Egypt), whose last lot of gladiators were very poor, a hamstrung crew you could have blown over. No wonder they were flogged afterwards for their feeble performance.

Here then is a fascinating glimpse of local politics. Success for the candidates for office depends entirely on the support they win as the result of the shows they put on. On these alone are they judged by the townsfolk as persons and as politicians. The cynicism extends to the performers. Gladiators and condemned criminals, prisoners of war and desperate debtors are not thought of as human beings or, if so, the fact only increases the lust for cruelty in the spectators. Public morality is dead in this first century of the Christian era. Numerous followers of Christ are indeed alive and spreading the Gospel in these dreadful days at Puteoli as elsewhere in the Roman world, but they are still too few to influence the mass mind. They are regarded as a dangerous and vicious sect, given to magic practices and human sacrifice in their suspect secrecy. Above all they are disloyal to the god-emperor.

Echion is now in a grumbling mood. Petronius notes the volatility of these Greeklings. A minute ago he was an optimist, now he looks on the black side, just as Phileros bade his fellow guests be mindful of the living, only to talk of the dead. The clothes dealer imagines, no doubt correctly, that Agamemnon despises him as an ignorant fellow. However, he is willing to rise above it and to invite the rhetorician to come along one day for a meal and see his little protégé who is really keen on his letters. Echion wants him to study law or at least some trade, but law is best, it feeds a man. Just look at Phileros. He was a traveling salesman who studied law, and now he even enters the lists against Norbanus.

Thus a brief array of contemporary types, all drawn from the freedman milieu of small-town Campania, a perfect imitation of the real thing, based, we may be certain, upon men actually known to the author—men who had served and been freed upon his own estates and those of friends.

X *Chapters 47–52. Smelly Bronze and Unbreakable Glass*

Our host returns. By way of apology for his absence, he explains that his bowels have been troubling him of late. Various remedies have been suggested, but the doctors are puzzled. Right now his stomach rumbles, you'd think it a bull. He won't mind if any of his guests feel the need to relieve themselves by letting wind. Perhaps Petronius is thinking of a decree attributed, no doubt falsely, to Claudius, permitting a similar license at his own table. Fortunata has no right to laugh, she keeps him awake nights by doing the same thing. The guests express their thanks for this generous concession, hiding their smiles in their cups.

Pigs are now paraded adorned with caps and bells. One is chosen for the pot and Trimalchio resumes control of the conversation. The wine is from a new estate which he has not yet visited, between Tarracina (in Latium) and Tarentum (on the toe of Italy!). He intends furthermore to join Sicily to his bit of property so that he may travel through territory all his own on his way to Africa. Agamemnon is politely asked about his work but scarcely given a chance to reply, for Trimalchio is too keen to display his own erudition—Hercules, Ulysses, the Cyclops, all from Homer.

The pig returns from the kitchen apparently ungutted. The cook is stripped for punishment and ordered to gut it forthwith. He plys his knife and lo!—there falls out a stream of stuffing and sausages. The mock trial and its surprise dénouement are greeted with the usual applause. Again we see the craze for novelty, so relentlessly pursued by Trimalchio. The cook is rewarded with a silver garland and a goblet of Corinthian bronze, a highly prized and expensive gift. The donor makes the joke that it is Corinthian because the smith from whom he buys is called Corinthus! All the same, he knows the origin of Corinthian ware. When Troy(!) was captured, Hannibal melted down statues of bronze, silver, and gold to make a new amalgam—an interesting variant of the usual account involving Mummius, the taker of Corinth in 146 B.C.

Actually, Trimalchio prefers glassware to bronze, and so we are given a version of the story, popular at the time, of the invention of unbreakable glass, a discovery stifled at birth in order to preserve the industry. An artisan arrives at Tiberius' court with his specimen of the new glass. Admitted to the presence, he hands his gift to Caesar. Asking for it back, he lets it fall to the ground. Instead of breaking, it is merely dented. Whereupon the ingenious inventor straightens out the dent with a hammer, thinking that a handsome reward will be his. Unfortunately, the emperor has too much business sense, and fearing that for instance gold will be devalued by a sudden vogue for glass, orders the inventor to be beheaded.

It is likely that Petronius was concerned by the possibility of making unbreakable glass. The disadvantage of bronze vessels was that they had a smell which imparted itself to the contents. Hence the value of the murrine vase for which he paid so much,[3] it being made from some variety of fluorspar or jade obtained from Parthia and having a pleasing fragrance to impart. The subject must have aroused general interest, and the story told by Trimalchio is also told by Pliny (*Natural History,* 36, 195) and Dio Cassius (*Roman History,* 57, 21, 7). It is rather surprising to find it in the fictional *Satyricon,* unless we assume the author's personal preoccupation.

The witticism "Out with the water, in with the wine" meets with approval. Agamemnon in particular applauds, knowing how to secure another free meal sometime. Thus encouraged, the host gives his rendering of a performance by the mime actor Syrus, until restrained by Fortunata who urges him to respect the dignity of his position.

XI *Chapters 53–56. Affluence and Acrobats*

The huge estates of Trimalchio are sufficient to justify the compilation of a kind of newspaper report. One of Trimalchio's secretaries now reads out the events of "the 26th of July." The whole thing seems absurd, a piece of vulgar ostentation with some inconsistencies. The July date does not tally with the notice described in Chapter 30 as fixed to the dining-room door—"On the 30th and 31st of December the Master dines out." The report can hardly be for a half-year period, since each item is recorded as taking place on the same day (26th of July). Other seasonal discrepancies in the *Cena* are in Chapter 28 where the doorkeeper is shelling peas (the beginning of April?) and in Chapter 41 where Damas complains of the cold spell. This would fit April, but hardly late July. Obviously, we must not look for the consistency of realism in the *Satyricon.*

The account is first concerned with Trimalchio's estate at Cumae, which is of course not where the banquet is taking place. On the 26th of July then, thirty boys and forty girls have been born on the estate, fifteen hundred bushels of wheat stored in the barns, and five hundred oxen tamed for the plough. A slave Mithridates has been crucified for cursing his master's name, a million sesterces of spare cash put in the coffers. A fire has broken out in some pleasure gardens, the *horti Pompeiani.* Trimalchio is angry at this news. He had not been informed of the purchase of these gardens. They were acquired last year, says the secretary, and not yet entered on the books. Details follow of wills, penalties, and disputes. A steward has been banished to Baiae.

Enough is enough. Another novel item for dinner party procedure has been achieved, and certainly the guests will have been impressed both by the novelty and by the vastness of their host's possessions.

They are less impressed by the acrobats and jugglers which follow. A boy climbs a ladder, performs a song and dance at the top, then jumps through a burning hoop and finally holds up a seven-gallon jar in his teeth. Stale fare, but the master likes it and trumpeters too. As for comedians, he prefers them to perform Atellan plays rather than the Greek stuff. Here then, as with the hunting scene, he is affecting the interests of a gentleman. National drama was the perquisite of the men about town.[4] Greek plays were for the professional, a mere technician, not the true connoisseur of the theater.

The acrobats, however, are not such a tame performance as they seem. The boy falls from his ladder and injures Trimalchio's arm. Doctors come running and Fortunata, with hair disheveled, is preparing to assume the role of grief-stricken spouse, perhaps even widow. The guests are alarmed, not because they are anxious for the boy's safety—they would gladly see him break his neck—but because they would have to attend the funeral. Here again Petronius stresses the utter callousness of contemporary society. The boy meantime is going tbe round of the tables, begging the guests to intercede on his behalf.

Encolpius remembers the cook stripped for a flogging and suspects that the present accident is also a trick. His suspicions are increased when a servant receives a beating for using a white bandage instead of a purple one for his master's arm. Now comes the surprise: Trimalchio orders the boy to be declared free, lest it should be said that so important a person as himself has been injured by a slave.

This then is the length to which the host will go to amuse his guests. It is tantalizing for us in the twentieth century to try to decide how much verisimilitude there is in the *Satyricon.* The mentality of Trimalchio and his guests is absurd beyond our comprehension. But the world of Nero and his court, Petronius' world, is no less fantastic, if we are to believe its historians. How much of Trimalchio's banquet was surprising or shocking or funny and in what ways to Petronius' audience we cannot hope to assess correctly. The only thing we know definitely is that it was a satire on bad taste, but much of this satire too inevitably escapes us, separated as we are from the mind of the author and his listeners by nineteen hundred years.

The magnanimous master of the house cannot let the occasion pass without a few impromptu verses to mark it. This leads in the banquet tradition to a general discussion of poetry, illustrated by sixteen lines from the mime author Publilius Syrus,[5] an attack on the luxury and debauchery of the age, completely and deliberately out of keeping with Trimalchio's personality. Syrus was a favorite school-room manual in expurgated form, owing to the number and appositeness of his moral maxims. We may assume that our *nouveau-riche* had received a formal education from his one-time master. The use he makes of it is a dire comment on its futility. His mind is impervious to the sentiments he utters, and this imperviousness he shares with all but the most sensitive spirits of his age.

The spate of absurdities continues, embracing doctors, bankers, and dumb animals. Trimalchio is all set to put the philosophers out of business with his eloquence and wit, which culminate in a round of *apophoreta* where the humor lies in word play, the resemblance of the words of the mottoes to the object given away. This word play is one of the commonest devices of Latin colloquial humor. The plays of Plautus and Terence are rich in examples.[6]

XII *Chapters 57–61. Unseemly Mirth and Embarrassment*

At this point Ascyltos, whom we have not heard of since Chapter 24, when he was receiving the curative attentions of Quartilla, and who is now again the worse for wear, is making fun of everything and laughing till the tears come. The relative neglect of this character suggests that he is something of an embarrassment to his creator who suddenly remembers him after thirty-odd chapters as he will similarly remember Giton in Chapter 58. No doubt the intention has been to concentrate the spotlight upon Trimalchio and the other guests by way of variety.

One of the guests takes offence at this noisy mirth. Nerves must be pretty tense by now; no one knows what fresh and alarming surprise may be visited upon them by their exuberant host. The angry one is Hermeros, the neighbor whom Encolpius had consulted earlier about the identity of Fortunata and the meaning of certain strange dishes. He is an aggressive character and expresses himself in rich vernacular. He notices that Ascyltos is wearing a ring made of boxwood, the yellow color of which looks rather like gold. The latter is thus pretending to be a knight, and so Hermeros goes one better by claiming to be of royal descent.[7] Amid abuse of his victim, he continues to boast of his achievements, his credit, his thrift, and so on. He was a slave for fifty years, all of which time he conducted himself like a free man! He came as a long-haired slave boy to Puteoli, arriving there before the town hall was built.

Similar abuse is directed at Giton. It would seem that Hermeros, who proudly tells us that he has had only an elementary education, is all the same jealous of Ascyltos and Giton who are students of rhetoric. He tries to stump Giton with riddles—another popular pastime. It is interesting to see the resentment which some of the guests feel in the presence of the *scholastici* at dinner. We saw in Chapter 46 that Echion, the clothes dealer, was uneasy in the company of Professor Agamemnon.

Ascyltos and Giton are highly amused at the grossness and extravagance of Trimalchio. Encolpius we are to suppose is not so much amused as disgusted. He is of a more fastidious nature and is of course older than his companions, hence Giton's desertion of him for Ascyltos, younger and more virile. Thus the wandering trio, although quite disreputable in their way of life and not even above stealing, feel intellectually superior to the kind of freedman depicted in the *Cena*. Ascyltos is a freedman himself, and so we may assume are the other two. Their Greek names suggest this.

Trimalchio pours oil on troubled waters, and Homer players come on. The host reads a Latin version of the lines recited in Greek by the players. The implication that it is the gentlemanly thing to prefer the Latin is interesting. This Greco-Oriental community is anxious to identify itself as much as possible with the dominant power in the peninsula, even to the extent of affecting to despise the literature acknowledged by cultured Romans to be superior to their own. Petronius here puts his finger upon a common trait of human nature, to keep in with the powers that be. The Homer players are of course only a pretext. A boiled calf makes its appearance wearing a helmet. It is carved up by a mad Ajax and distributed to the diners.

After this exciting display of talent and culture, ironically described by Encolpius as "refined," the ornamental ceiling begins to rumble, shaking the whole room. Someone is up there, maybe an acrobat. All eyes are turned heavenwards and, behold, the heavens open, or rather the ceiling slides apart, and a huge circular hoop, taken from a barrel, is lowered down. Golden garlands and little alabaster ointment boxes hang from it—more gifts to take home.

The next trick takes the form of a tray holding a pastry figure of

Priapus, supporting a large quantity of various fruits upon the generous appendage with which he is traditionally represented. When touched, these fruits spread forth a spray of saffron essence, not altogether pleasant in excess. A dish so perfumed must have ceremonial significance, so we all stood up, says Encolpius, to sing God save the emperor. However, the moment of awe passes and the guests help themselves to the fruit, sacred or not. Encolpius does the same, mindful of Giton, his favorite. It must have been Trimalchio's intention to create a religious atmosphere, for little figures of the household gods (*lares*) are brought in, and various lucky charms, and finally a statuette of the master, reverently kissed by all.

No doubt this scene was a regular feature at a Roman dinner party. The guests were called upon to pay their respects, first to the emperor who was saluted as the Father of his Country, then to the guardian spirits of the house, whose blessing was invoked. The charms were figures of Good Luck, Profit, and so on. But the statuette of the *pater familias* is in less commendable taste.

After a generous "God bless us all," Trimalchio turns his attention to a guest who has hitherto had nothing to say for himself. "You used to be better company, but now you are silent, not a peep out of you. Come on, tell us of your big adventure." Apparently Niceros has shared the general embarrassment of the self-made businessman in the presence of the students of the School of Rhetoric. After all, they are supposed to be the experts in the art of speaking. It must be observed that Encolpius has had nothing to say for himself at the party, while Ascyltos and Giton by their unseemly mirth have merely roused resentment, instead of making a notable contribution to the conversation as *scholastici,* the purpose for which they were invited. Even Professor Agamemnon, the senior member of the party, has had almost nothing to say, merely repeating, when asked to do so, the theme of his day's declamation in the schoolroom—"A poor man and a rich man were enemies" (Chapter 48). It is true that Trimalchio interrupted him with a mock request for a definition—"What is a poor man?"—a joke which brought the house down and drowned poor Agamemnon's efforts. The fact remains that the scholars have put up a poor show.

Is this an oversight on Petronius' part? Or does he wish to show that Encolpius and his friends are equally embarrassed? I think the latter is the right explanation. If so, we have an indication that the scholars are misfits in the freedman society to which they belong. This explains their wandering status. They have been educated above their station and do not possess the strength of character or purpose to forge a career in literature, law or politics, to become, like Pallas or Narcissus, powers to be reckoned with. Perhaps they are still too young. More likely, they are intellectual independents, constitutional *satyricoi.*

Niceros pointedly remarks on his embarrassment. "Let's be merry, even though I am afraid those student types will laugh at me. That's their lookout. I'll tell my tale all the same. They can't rob me of anything, it's better to be laughed at than laughed down!" He is encouraged by his host and launches into a fascinating tale, pure folklore, an element rightly introduced into this lighthearted romance to the eternal gratitude of the centuries to come.

XIII *Chapters 61–63. Folklore*

The scene of the tale is presumably Puteoli, in a narrow quarter of the town. When Niceros was a slave at a house now occupied by one Gavilla, there was an attractive young lady in service there too. She is now the wife of Terence the innkeeper. You all knew her, he says, her name was Melissa and she came from Tarentum, a charming piece of goods. But it wasn't her physique I was really interested in. I wasn't after sex, you understand. It was her good nature which won me. She was so generous, always sharing what she earned with me. She saved it up for me and never cheated me. It so happened that her mate died while they were both doing a spell of service away at the master's country home. So I raised heaven and earth to get out there to her.

It chanced that the master had gone off to Capua to sell some odds and ends. So I persuaded a chap who was staying with us to come along with me as far as the fifth milestone. He was a soldier —strong as the devil.

We cleared off at cockcrow. The moon was shining like broad daylight. We arrived among the tombstones, and soldier boy began to relieve himself up against a monument.

Niceros sits waiting, humming to himself, and counting the tombstones. At last he looks up and sees his companion undressing himself and laying his clothes beside the road. As Niceros watches, heart in mouth, the soldier makes water round the pile of clothes (a homely version of a magic protective circle), suddenly changes into a wolf and flees howling into the woods. The clothes had turned to stone.

Panic-stricken, Niceros takes up the sword which the soldier had left behind, and hacks away at the shadows, real or imaginary, along the roadside until he arrives at the farm where his girl friend is in service. He enters the house, looking like a ghost, the sweat pouring down. Melissa wonders why he is so late. "If you'd come earlier, you could have been of some help. A wolf just came in to the farmyard and slaughtered all the beasts like a man from the abattoir. All the same he didn't get away with it. A slave ran him through the neck with a spear."

After a sleepless night, Niceros clears off home with his tail between his legs. When he reaches the spot where the soldier had changed his identity, there was nothing but a pool of blood. And when he got home, there was the fellow lying on his bed like a felled ox with the doctor looking at his neck. I knew then that he was a werewolf, and I couldn't eat a bite in his company after that.

It is not possible to trace the origin of this story which is certainly not the work solely of Petronius' imagination, although the details of the setting and names of the characters are probably his own. He may have heard the main facts of the story from a friend or servant, perhaps on his Campanian estate. It is unlikely that he brought the tale back with him from Bithynia, the probable source of the Milesian tales, equally of popular origin, of which we have examples elsewhere in the *Satyricon,* although of course some of these, compiled by Aristides of Miletus, had been translated by the Roman Sisenna (p. 42). It may be noted, however, that Petronius' two *Milesiaca* are both recounted by Eumolpus, who is a man of letters, whereas our present werewolf story is told by a real man of the people, without any literary pretensions. It is probably a pure example of an age-old oral tradition, not yet consigned to a literary genre like the Milesians.

Not to be outdone, Trimalchio also relates a weird experience. While he was still a long-haired slave boy (hence his sentimental attachment to them now), his master's favorite died, a pearl of a boy and very intelligent. The child's mother was weeping over him, and suddenly witches began their hideous screeching. A tough giant of a Cappadocian drew his sword, ran out of the house, and pierced one of them through the middle. But his whole body became black and blue as though he had been flogged, for the witch had touched him with her evil hand. The mother found her son's body filched away and a straw dummy put in its place. The Cappadocian never recovered and a few days later died, raving mad.

Encolpius' comment is curious. "We wonder at the tale and believe it no less." Trimalchio is convinced: "There are women of supernatural powers, creatures of the night, and they turn things upside down." All kiss the table and make a prayer that the witches keep themselves to themselves while the guests go home after the dinner. Encolpius is probably ironical, reflecting Petronius' own skepticism regarding all such superstitions, the same spirit in which he attacked the rites of Priapus.

XIV *Chapters 64–70. A Dog Fight, a Drunk, and Damaged Virgil*

Another guest, Plocamus, has also been silent. He used to be a good singer. He answers that he is past his prime and suffering from gout. In past years he rivaled Apelles (perhaps the actor famous under Caligula; cf. Suetonius, *Caligula,* 33) in singing, dancing, and comic turns.

We are now treated to a diversion with a lapdog called Pearl belonging to Croesus, Trimalchio's favorite boy, and a mastiff of huge proportions, "the guardian of house and home," answering to the name of Tiny (Scylax). The two are urged to fight with consequent chaos and a smashing of the crystal ware. More food is served, only capons and goose eggs, much to Encolpius' disgust; he had expected thrushes at least.

At this point a belated reveler breaks in upon the company. This is a convention of the symposium genre (e.g., Alcibiades' entry in Plato, *Symposium,* 212D). He is dressed in white robes and has quite an array of attendants. Encolpius is impressed and thinks the local governor (praetor) has arrived. But Agamemnon recognizes a minor official by the name of Habinnas the stonemason, who now installs himself in the place of honor, supporting himself upon his wife's shoulders and wreathed in festive garlands with perfume running down into his eyes. He has just come from another party given by one Scissa, who is giving a celebration for her deceased slave boy, manumitted on his deathbed, a not uncommon practice.

Habinnas obliges with an account of what he has had for dinner, the *pièce de résistance* was bear meat, which, says he, tastes like boar. But his wife Scintilla ("Little Spark") nearly spewed up her guts over it.

"Where is Fortunata?" asks Habinnas, remembering his party manners. "Putting away the silver and dividing up the remains of the food among the slaves," replies the host. Habinnas won't stay if she doesn't show up, so she is summoned, all dressed up in a tunic of cerise with a yellow waistband. Trimalchio's taste for bright colors is shared by his wife. She has gold-embroidered slippers too.

Fortunata falls into the arms of Scintilla and the two begin to gossip and show off their jewelry. Habinnas tips up Fortunata on to the couch and she blushes furiously, hiding her shame in Scintilla's bosom. So much for the conduct of a local magistrate in society, implies our author. Habinnas' language too is of the crudest, and it is likely that Petronius has some personage in mind whom he has met in convivial Campania. It is true that Scintilla was complaining to Fortunata about her husband's attentions to his mignon and his consequent neglect of herself.

The tables are now removed, and the dining-room floor, which must by this time have been in a highly disordered condition, is sprinkled with powder colored with saffron and minium. Even here a novelty is introduced, for the powder is mingled with ground mica to give a shiny effect. Trimalchio draws attention to the fact by remarking that the mixture looks good enough to eat.

An Alexandrian slave boy does an imitation of nightingales and an attendant of Habinnas begins to recite from Virgil's *Aeneid*. The attendant is untrained for epic and uses a stress accent which gives a discordant effect to the Latin verses. Presumably a pitch accentuation in imitation of Greek practice was considered correct for epic meter. Moreover, the wretched youth imparts an Atellan flavor to Virgil by getting his quantities wrong, so that the stately spondaic rhythm is marred by too many shortened syllables, recalling the quick-moving satyric hexameter of popular farce.

"He never had formal instruction," says Habinnas unnecessarily, "I sent him to the strollers." The latter, *circulatores* as the Romans called them, were itinerant performers in the popular tradition, purveyors of oral tales (like the *raconteurs* of the streets of Paris even today) who also gave imitations and did acrobatics. Once again then we see that vogue for the national product which prompted Trimalchio's preference for a Latin text of Homer in Chapter 59. Petronius as a *satyricos* could not have been unsympathetic, but he draws the line at contaminating Virgil.

Scintilla is inclined to be jealous of Habinnas' praises of his boy performer, but Trimalchio reminds her that they all know her too. Encouraged by this remark, the boy proceeds to give further items from his repertory, including an imitation of mule-drivers. These were the long-distance truck drivers of antiquity, and their varied experiences among different peoples in many lands made them a favorite subject for caricature in mime and farce.

Still more food, apparently stuffed goose, fish, and game. But it's all made out of one substance, says Trimalchio. Encolpius has seen this sort of thing before. "I shouldn't be surprised if it's all made out of excrement or perhaps mud," he remarks. "They do it at the Saturnalia."

But no. It's all made out of pork. The expert cook fashions a fish from a sow's udder, and with lard he makes a dove, and so on. Trimalchio has given him a suitable name, Daedalus, after the legendary inventor of arts and crafts. More tricks and then a bit of disgusting oriental practice. The guests have their feet washed in perfumed oil from a silver basin.

XV *Chapters 71–78. Ad Nauseam*

Things now decline into a general debacle. Fortunata and Scintilla are getting out of hand. Trimalchio completes the chaos by inviting the slaves to take their place at table. Even they are accomplished in the arts of the *palaestra,* for the ingenious cook who makes things out of pork now begins an imitation of a tragic player Ephesus (unknown) and lays a bet with his master as to the prospects of the "Greens" at the next chariot races.[8] Thus a temporary freedom is accorded to the servants such as obtained by general custom at the time of the Saturnalia in December.

Trimalchio proclaims that slaves are human beings, victims of malicious fate. He intends to free in his will all those of his immediate household and to one or two he will leave property. Fortunata is to inherit his estates and he commends her to all his friends. Then he orders a copy of his will to be brought and read out. We are spared the details but the whole company, we are told, groans in unison at the recital. Then he gives instructions to Habinnas (we remember that he is a mason) about the monument he is to build, depicting a lapdog at his master's feet, the garlands and unguent boxes of festivity, and also all the fights of the pugilist Petraites (unknown). Other details are to represent him as a magistrate wearing his robes and fine gold rings, as distributing largesse to the multitude and as the donor of a public banquet. There are to be statues of Fortunata holding a dove and his favorite boy weeping over a broken urn. Even a sundial is included. The inscription is to record his achievements and the fact that he left thirty million and never went to college.

The thought of all this overcomes him, and he bursts into tears in which the assembly dutifully join him, flooding the house with lamentation. But Trimalchio is volatile. He bids his guests rouse themselves and repair to the bathhouse. Habinnas likes the idea of making two days out of one, as the bath was considered the beginning of a day of revelry. The intention then is to start all over again. The wheel has turned full cycle. The prospect is too hideous for Encolpius, and we sense that Petronius also has had enough. He now prepares to wind up the banquet episode, which he does in six more chapters.

The students decide to slip away unseen as the crowd makes for the bathhouse. But in this they are thwarted. A watchdog posted by the exit frightens them with its frantic barking and Ascyltos falls into a pond. Encolpius is pulled in too while trying to rescue him. The majordomo fishes them out and they are compelled to follow through with the rest of the guests. Trimalchio's hospitality has to be paid for by enduring his company to the bitter end. The ordeal of the bath is made worse by the host's determined rendering of the songs of Menecrates (Suetonius, *Nero,* 30), a well-known artist of the day.

Their drunken stupor washed away, the guests are escorted to another dining room, more elaborately furnished than the previous one, with silver tables and cups inlaid with gold. The occasion for this celebration is the ceremonial first cutting of the beard by one of Trimalchio's slaves, a custom made much of by the Romans as a kind of coming of age.[9]

The intention is to feast until the dawn. But dawn is already at hand, for a cock crows. Trimalchio is disturbed by this apparent omen. Does he think they are still in the middle of the night? Wine is poured under the table and even the lamps are sprinkled with it to avert evil. He changes his ring from left hand to right. It means a fire or some death in the neighborhood. But a cock is brought and put in the pot. Is it all a trick?

The first round of slaves has finished eating. A second team takes their place. A brawl breaks out between Fortunata and her husband when he makes for a handsome slave boy and plasters him with kisses. Trimalchio seizes a cup and throws it in her face, following this injury with a volley of abuse. Fortunata is an ungrateful wretch after all he has done for her, and so on. He won't have her statue by his tomb, after all; nay more, she shall not be allowed to kiss his dead body.

Petronius shows how ugly can be the final stages of a party given by such people. He has prolonged the episode ad nauseam in order to disgust an audience paradoxically capable of far worse disorders. The message can only be that there is no limit to human hypocrisy—let us recognize it in ourselves, a message potentially dangerous, but, as we have seen, Petronius was no coward.

At last, the host allows himself to be pacified, although he is still angry. Why is Fortunata so jealous? The boy is honest, conscientious, and intelligent. We learn that Trimalchio was for fourteen years his master's mignon. He came as a young boy from Asia, in fact a mere child who used to measure himself against a candelabrum and smear his cheeks with lamp oil to make his beard come faster.

Further details: how he gradually imposed himself upon his master's will and secured his inheritance—a handsome fortune. But he was ambitious for more and so went into business, building a fleet of ships which he loaded with wine and sent to Rome. The lot went down, wiping out at one blow thirty million. Nothing daunted, he started again with more and bigger ships with cargoes of wine, meat, vegetables, perfumes, and slaves, an interesting light upon the trade done by the Bay of Naples ports.

Fortunata did a good job here. She sold all her clothes and jewels to give him the hundred gold pieces that became the nucleus of his present fortune. In one voyage he cleared up ten million. He bought up his former master's property, built a new house, and got slaves and livestock. Then he went into banking, financing newly freed slaves to get them started in a trade.

A fortune-teller gave him good advice, warning him against being too generous—he was nursing a viper in his bosom. He was told he is to live another thirty years, four months, and two days, a precision which is a common feature of inscriptions upon Roman tombstones. He now aims to join Apulia to his estates—before it was Sicily (Chapter 48). His present home has four dining rooms, twenty bedrooms, two porticoes, and so on.

Another sentimental death-bed rehearsal. Trumpeters are summoned and Trimalchio is conveyed to the dining room stretched out upon a couch as though in death. The undertaker's boy makes such a din of lamentation that the fire brigade, doing duty in the neighborhood, think the house is on fire. They break down the door and start to ply their axes and throw water everywhere. Encolpius, Ascyltos, and Giton take the opportunity to escape, leaving Agamemnon to his fate.

We too breathe a sigh of relief. Petronius has wrung the uttermost effect from his travesty of the banquet genre. Only the wealth of realistic detail and the exciting rapidity of the narrative have saved the recital from becoming too tedious. If the intention was to build up an effect of impatience and disgust at the vainglorious host and his incessant lapses from good taste, then we shall say our author has succeeded. It is true that the *Satyricon* was composed to be read aloud in serial form to a selected audience, certainly by the author himself, who with his consummate artistry could convey all the nuances intended. The exquisite irony of many a detail which escapes us because of our imperfect knowledge of the contemporary scene would be rendered by intonation, meaningful pause, and all the other devices of a skilled exponent. Furthermore, the atmosphere of conviviality in which the narrative was delivered must have added greatly to its success. The present-day silent and solitary reader is hampered by the gap of centuries and his vastly different environment. To read the *Satyricon* one ought ideally to be a *satyricos*. But we enjoy it in spite of our inhibitions.

XVI *Chapters 79–87. Eumolpus, Art, and Hypocrisy*

Chapter 79 brings us back to the same narrow streets that led astray Encolpius and Ascyltos in Chapters 6 and 8. Thus the *Cena* episode takes place in the same town, Puteoli, as the Priapic episode with Quartilla, a town to which our wandering students are strangers. The *stabulum* or lodging house referred to in Chapter 79 is the same as that of Chapters 6 and 8. The fact is important as it indicates clearly that the first three sections of the *Satyricon* as we have it (Chapters 26 to 99 inclusive) are closely linked. It is unlikely therefore that the complete work was much longer than the present version, for Chapter 100 finds our heroes on board the ship which they entered in Chapter 99 and from which they are rescued in Chapter 124 by fishermen who land them on the coast near Croton, the scene of the remaining chapters of the book. If our surviving fragments belong to only one section of a much larger compilation, it is indeed surprising that we have no traces of the other sections. The odd quotations in prose attributed to Petronius which we find in later writers like Fulgentius and Isidore seem to refer to incidents which we possess. The longer verse fragments which these writers give are more difficult to place and more probably belong to the corpus of Petronius' writings independent of the *Satyricon*.

Once back at their lodgings, Encolpius enjoys the favors of Giton until, relaxed in wine and sleep, he looses his embrace upon the boy. Whereupon Ascyltos filches him away to his own bed.

The situation reverts to what it was in Chapter 10 when the students decided to part company next day, since in the evening they were invited to Trimalchio's. The dinner party has lasted throughout the night and now it is early morning. Their meager goods are duly shared out but they cannot agree to divide up the boy; so they prepare to fight a duel, Giton meantime beseeching them to abstain from mutual slaughter. Wisdom prevails. Ascyltos suggests that Giton choose between them. Encolpius agrees, thinking that his long association with Giton will decide the issue in his favor. But Giton chooses—Ascyltos! Priapus must still be angry with Encolpius, robbing him of his power to please.

Abandoned, he leaves the lodging house and moves down to the beach, there to indulge his grief in flights of rhetoric, condemning the two offenders, promising himself revenge. His imagination is so worked up that he girds a sword and rushes forth to seek them, only to be accosted by a soldier who challenges his identity, seeing him armed, and confiscates the sword, letting him off this time with a caution.

Thus ends Chapter 82. A gap in the narrative occurs and Chapter 83 finds Encolpius in a picture gallery, in rapt admiration before the paintings of such masters as Zeuxis, Protogenes, and Apelles (all fourth century B.C.). The artists have chosen as their themes incidents from the love life of the gods, and Encolpius is moved to envy by these divine dallyings among mortals, which he contrasts with his own privation in such matters.

An old man enters the gallery. A rather impressive figure with a shock of white hair and a dignified though ravaged countenance. A man of letters certainly but whose neglected, poverty-stricken attire proclaims that he does not enjoy the patronage of the wealthy. He addresses himself to Encolpius, proclaiming himself a poet, and obviously he does not share the world's poor opinion of himself. He is a true lover of art for art's sake and without more ado breaks forth into half a dozen verses to prove his talents, following up with a tirade against the base materialism of the rich by way of contrast with himself whose genius and integrity of life make him their natural enemy.

This is our first introduction to Eumolpus, the beggar poet and philosopher who plays such a large part in the ensuing action. Indeed, from now on he replaces Ascyltos as Encolpius' companion and tends to overshadow the younger man's rather obscure personality. We soon discover him to be a complete sham, whose lofty sentiments are the barest camouflage for the mind of a dirty old man. A number of lacunae mar the text at this point, and it would seem that the epitomist has thought it necessary to expurgate some of the newcomer's conversation. He has, however, preserved for us, though not entirely, the scabrous but fascinating account of Eumolpus' seduction of a young boy at Pergamum, the son of one of the inhabitants at whose house Eumolpus, then in military service, was billeted.

The story bears the ingredients of the genre known as Milesian, and, as has been suggested, Petronius may have brought back the essence of it from Bithynia. But he treats this essence in his own inimitable way with his usual delicious irony and felicity of phrasing. He puts the tale into the mouth of Eumolpus, whose character it suits to perfection as a consummate master of philosophical bombast and hypocrisy. Our author's manner of telling this little incident brings out the amazing similarity between his technique and Voltaire's. A remark like the following, from Chapter 85: "Whenever the conversation at table touched upon the abuse of young boys, I blazed forth with indignation, refusing to allow my ears to be polluted with such obscene discussion, so that the mother in particular began to look upon me as a true philosopher" comes straight from a *conte* by the Frenchman.

Surely a Petronian invention is the boy's complete readiness to be seduced, so that he begins to snore, having overheard, for he was not asleep, Eumolpus' prayer to Venus that he may enjoy the boy's favors while he sleeps unawares. The fact is that the boy is already corrupt and Eumolpus is probably not the first comer on the scene—a typically Petronian touch of cynicism. Indeed, it is difficult to decide who is the more hypocritical of the two, the seducer or the seduced. Eumolpus goes through the same rigmarole of prayer to Venus on the next night, although he knows the boy is listening and only too willing, while concealing the fact.

This Milesian tale is then a ruthless presentation of hypocrisy and corruption, relieved or perhaps, according to the reader's temperament, aggravated by a cynical playfulness of treatment. So too is the other example, the story of the Widow of Ephesus, told in Chapters 111 and 112, also by Eumolpus. From the Petronian point of view the moral in both cases would seem to be this: sexual desire is at once powerful and natural. Why not admit it and be candid in the expression of such desire?

Certainly, this theme of hypocrisy is much in evidence in the *Satyricon*. Most of the characters are tainted with it, not least Encolpius, Ascyltos, and Giton in their dealings with each other. It is strongly marked in the women also, be they housewives or self-styled priestesses. The subject is dear to the Romans, whether satirists or historians. It is a trait of the Roman character. The most eloquent denouncers of hypocrisy in society, Sallust and Seneca, were themselves hypocrites of no mean order.

Above all, it must not be supposed that Petronius considered the vice confined to the lower classes. The death-bed document he posted to Nero spoke out at last to a court he could not, as he valued his life until compelled to end it, condemn before.

XVII *Chapters 88–99. Poetry, Melodrama, and Good-bye Puteoli*

There now follows a discussion of the decline in artistic achievement. Painting in fact has ceased to exist. Greed for money is the reason for this. In bygone days, virtue reigned supreme. Men thought only of what would benefit posterity and devoted their lives to that end. Hence the achievements of the Greek scientists and artists. We in the present age are sunk in debauchery, having absorbed only the vices of the past and none of its virtues. Wealth alone is sought and prayed for. A heap of gold is considered more beautiful than anything wrought by Apelles or Phidias.

Thus speaks Eumolpus, the voice of hypocrisy, echoing sentiments which are a commonplace in Latin literature. We are particularly reminded of Sallust's opening remarks in the *Catiline*.

We are of course still in the picture gallery and Encolpius is now examining a painting which has for its subject the capture of Troy. The occasion is too good to miss and Eumolpus breaks into sixty-five iambic senarii anent the wooden horse and its fatal contents, sparing us no detail of rhetoric and imagery.

The theme is topical. Nero had himself handled it, as befitting one divinely descended from the royal house of Troy. Put into Eumolpus' mouth, the present rendering must be a parody, how not to go about the subject. Tragic simplicity and realism are sacrificed to exaggeration and artificiality. We must assume that Nero approved and that there was nothing in our author's example to arouse his resentment. At any rate, we are left in no doubt about the bystanders' reaction to the recital. They hurl stones at Eumolpus, who hastily retreats from the gallery which is situated, we learn, in the portico of a temple. Encolpius fears that he too may be taken for a poet and also takes to his heels.

Once the two are safely out of range, Encolpius asks his companion what is the matter with him that he talks more like a poet than a human being? He too will have to protect himself against Eumolpus' creative flights by keeping a reserve of stones. The other is unmoved by the rebuke; indeed he is used to such treatment—he volunteers the statement with melancholy pride—every time he enters the theater to give a recital, this is the reception he gets. However, he promises to behave himself at least for the rest of the day and Encolpius takes him to a hotel to buy him a meal.

They enter the bathhouse of the establishment and behold—there is Giton, repentant and disillusioned over Ascyltos. Reunited, the lovers give Eumolpus the slip—he is still reciting poetry in his bath—and repair to Encolpius' lodging where, amid tears and mutual reproaches, they are reconciled to each other's embraces.

Alas, they are not left long in peace. They are just about to enjoy a meal when a knock comes at the door. Eumolpus has arrived. Encolpius is reassured. He had feared that it might be Ascyltos at the door. But his confidence is ill-timed, for Eumolpus, as he should have remembered, has an eye for young boys.

No sooner does he take his seat upon the bed than our poet begins to admire the beauty of Giton doing a Ganymede and serving the drinks. It appears that he was expelled by popular outcry from the bathhouse, for reciting verse. All the admiration was for a young man (none other than Ascyltos) who had lost his clothes and whose nakedness displayed natural advantages to win all hearts. A Roman knight adopts him, clothes him and takes him home. Encolpius has difficulty in hiding his resentment at his former friend's good fortune.

This last admission is significant. It shows that Encolpius would be as ready to submit himself to the same infamous patronage as does Ascyltos. Hitherto we have seen him in a more favorable light, as a loyal and genuinely loving protector of an ungrateful Giton. But apparently he is quite unscrupulous in matters of sexual conduct, and, indeed, later on we see him prepared to extend his favors even to the ladies. He is in fact as completely devoid of moral sense as Eumolpus. Both appear to be shiftless and idle opportunists, preferring freedom to responsibility. In Eumolpus we see what Encolpius, unless he has special talents, will eventually become. Encolpius is a student of rhetoric and the arts, so must Eumolpus have been in youth. The latter has been described as of rather impressive physical appearance (Chapter 83) and as a boy no doubt served in Giton's capacity as a mignon, a state which Encolpius still hankers after.

Eumolpus' talent as a poet is unremarkable, but he is no worse than the average versifier of an age soaked in rhetoric and by and large incapable of genuine feeling. He is unfortunate in not having a patron, perhaps because his transparent dishonesty is repellent. Meanwhile he has a real gift of graceful and elegant discourse. Encolpius also declaims verse on occasion, when emotionally aroused. The practice will degenerate in him also into an uncontrollable vice when he no longer has the fervor of youth to justify his outbursts.

The beggar poet is the most important character in the *Satyricon* after Encolpius himself. He is more important than Trimalchio, for the latter is not really part of the framework of the action, but merely the protagonist of a single episode which is, and has been made by the epitomist, detachable from the main fabric. This being the case, we see how Eumolpus is both a foil to Encolpius as a bore and a threat to his love life and also a complement to him, inasmuch as he is the younger man's spiritual father. The picture is not an edifying one. We should suspect a moral purpose were it not for the fact that Petronius' own life and that of his circle was even more disreputable than anything in the *Satyricon.*

The true vocation after all of both Eumolpus and Encolpius is the pursuit of the pleasures which Venus and her grotesque offspring Priapus offer to Mankind. In this they are at one with Quartilla, with Giton, with Circe, whom we shall meet later, and with several of the minor characters. It is the lawful activity of the human race, says our author, himself mainly dedicated to the same end, the end prescribed by Epicurus the Wise. Repeatedly the message comes through, to follow one's natural inclinations is not immoral. The immorality of the characters consists in their hypocrisy in concealing, albeit under pressure of circumstances, their real motives. Petronius extends this hypocrisy to any strait-laced critics of his work, the would-be censorious Catos condemned in the verses of Chapter 132.

Partly to console himself for his reverse in the bathhouse, Eumolpus launches into philosophical hendecasyllabics. Our jaded appetites seek only exotic fare. The good things which are familiar no longer appeal. The verses are hardly attractive, the sentiments commonplace. We are exasperated and Encolpius is too. "Is this your promise not to versify today? Have pity on us, we have thrown you no stones. Think of what happened in the picture gallery and in the baths. If anyone in the house hears you, we shall all be put outside!"

Giton, shocked by this reproof to an older person, scolds Encolpius for his lack of manners and hospitality. These generous sentiments enhance the charm of the youngster. Indeed he has an affectionate disposition and seems genuinely sorry, for instance, to have come between Encolpius and Ascyltos.

Eumolpus is not slow in trying to profit by the boy's solicitude. He overwhelms him with compliments and informs him that he has found a lover who will fill books of verse with his praises.Our poet is completely insensitive. We can imagine Giton shuddering at the idea. And then, to cap it all, he calmly adds, "Encolpius will not be the loser, for he loves another." This piece of impertinence rouses the just wrath of the other, who with unconscious irony denounces the poet as a loose liver and angrily shows him the door. Giton meantime has made himself scarce, on the pretext of going to fetch water. The lecherous old man, however, is cunning as well as cowardly. He at once leaves the apartment, but banging the door behind him, he locks it at the same time and leaves poor Encolpius a prisoner, while he runs off to find Giton.

The situation is too much for our hero. He decides to put an end to his wretched existence by the rope, or rather by a noose made out of his girdle strung on to the bed frame. Before the fatal moment, however, the door is opened again, and Eumolpus returns with Giton. The latter is distracted with grief at his beloved's plight and a scene of mock heroics ensues. The boy seizes a razor from Eumolpus' servant and, striking his throat, collapses at the feet of his companions. Encolpius does a Juliet to Giton's Romeo and strikes himself with the same weapon. The tragedy turns to farce, for the razor is a dummy one, used for teaching novice barbers their trade.

Petronius refers to this incident as a theatrical entertainment, using the terms mime and fabula, and indeed the scene which now follows is pure knockabout farce in the Atellan tradition.

"What are you clowning at?" cries the lodging-house keeper who is just arriving with a tray of food. What roles, he says in effect, have you chosen for yourselves, that of drunks or of runaway slaves, or both at once? Here is a reference to two of the stock parts in Italian farce, parts which Plautus contrives to bring into his plays for comic effect. He accuses them of planning a midnight getaway without paying for their quarters. A fight ensues—the innkeeper throws an earthenware jar at Eumolpus who retaliates by beating the other's head with a candlestick. We are reminded of the brawl at the end of the *Cena*. Encolpius shuts the door on Eumolpus.

The fighting continues outside the door with cooks and boarders belaboring Eumolpus. A hideous old woman (another stock character of farce) sets a huge dog on him, but he defends himself with his candlestick. Through a hole in the door Encolpius enjoys the sight of the poet's discomfiture. Giton again shows a kindly feeling and argues that they should open the door and go to the rescue. Possibly Petronius wishes to indicate that the boy, because of his tender years, has not yet acquired the callousness which experience of life has conferred upon his seniors.

This time Encolpius will not let himself be influenced and boxes Giton's ears for interrupting. The result of course is that the boy collapses on the bed in tears. All this is the convention of farce, and we see how much a naughty but attractive child can contribute to an amusing situation.

At this point the manager of the apartment house intervenes. Here is another richly comic figure. Gout-ridden, he is conveyed upon the scene in a litter by two attendants and proceeds to bawl out the disputants in high fury. Then he catches sight of Eumolpus and the two are no strangers to each other. Apparently Bargates, the manager, is an admirer of Eumolpus. He is scandalized that the "worthless slaves" should brawl thus in his presence. We get a glimpse here of the poet's true milieu. He is a tavern performer, the precursor of many such who meet us in medieval literature. "Incidentally," says Bargates, "my missus is giving me trouble with her sauce. Take her down a peg in some of your verses and do me a favor."

A town crier enters the building and announces the offer of a reward, a thousand pieces of silver, for the recovery of Giton. It is Ascyltos who makes the offer, and he stands beside the crier with the money on a platter. Giton, at Encolpius' bidding, gets under the bed and hangs on to the wires of the mattress, like Ulysses under the sheep's belly.

Ascyltos goes the round of the apartments and arrives in due course at Encolpius' door. His suspicions aroused, he orders the crier's attendant to break down the door with his axe. In desperate subterfuge, Encolpius falls on his knees and beseeches his former friend to let him see Giton. How this is to be accomplished is not clear, since the boy is supposed to be missing. He pretends to think that Ascyltos has come to kill him. But Ascyltos bears no ill will; he is merely in search of his "runaway slave." With this remark he disappears.

Poor Giton, overcome with the dust beneath the bed, sneezes and reveals his presence to Eumolpus. Once more he is reduced to acting the peacemaker, blaming himself for causing all this trouble between friends. There is a repetition of the scene in Chapter 80 where he begged Encolpius and Ascyltos to slay him, the curse of both their lives, only this time Eumolpus has replaced

Ascyltos. At moments like this, one feels the burden of the serial story, a certain tediousness in recurrent situations which tends to mark the picaresque novel.

The truth of the matter is this: the protagonists are too limited as characterizations. Ascyltos is a shadowy figure whose morals are an exact counterpart of Encolpius' own. Apart from them, he is nonexistent. Encolpius has a certain life; his irony makes him amusing, but we can have too much of it and he has nothing else to offer. Giton is more vivid, but his repertory is meager—cajoling charm, modesty, and gentleness, the nicer sides of his promiscuous temperament. On occasion he is resourceful, cooking meals or finding his way by chalk marks through unfamiliar streets. Eumolpus is a much more developed personality, although an irritating one who inflicts his noxious being upon the others all the more devastatingly because they are rather negative and passive. Encolpius' fits of anger only accentuate his helplessness against a more cunning and experienced rival.

Giton sets the pace for a general reconciliation. This device of peacemaking, one realizes, is to clear the way for new adventures, to extricate the characters from a situation which has degenerated beyond further exploitation. Petronius must carry on the narrative for the next evening's recital at Nero's dinner table.

It would seem that the author has taken the opportunity to get rid of the least satisfactory of his characters. When Ascyltos hurries off at the end of Chapter 97 to continue his search for Giton, we are to see him no more. It is unnecessary to have two foils to Encolpius, and the beggar poet is retained instead of Ascyltos as being a more successful creation. We have had him with us since Chapter 83, and it has become increasingly difficult, with his advent, to fit Ascyltos into the action. When present, he tends to dominate the scene. He was an embarrassment to the lovers' triangle constituted by Encolpius, Ascyltos, and Giton. With the departure of Ascyltos, the triangular structure is resumed and more effectively. Instead of two young men and a boy, we have a young man, an old man, and a boy, each of the trio contrasting with the other two and all united by the common trait of homosexuality.

All the same this final departure of Ascyltos is too abrupt. We have not been prepared for it. On the contrary, Ascyltos' remark that he retains all his old affection for his former companion suggests that the two will resume their relationship later on. There is every indication that Petronius made a sudden change of plan for his work in order to avoid tedium, possibly at the suggestion of a friend who read the manuscript prior to its formal recital.

The decision was made to bring events at Puteoli to an end and to effect a complete change of setting. The change is made skillfully enough, but is nevertheless very abrupt. Eumolpus and Encolpius are reconciled and decide to shift their quarters, accompanied by Giton. "Follow me," says the poet, "or, if you will, take the lead and I will follow." Suddenly the initiative is taken from both of them. There is a knock at the door, and a bearded sailor confronts them. "Hurry up," he says to Eumolpus, "you know we must get moving." But there was no indication that Eumolpus did know. And suddenly they all go on board ship, whither bound we know not and neither, we feel, do they. Petronius tries to remedy this defect of procedure in Chapter 101 by making Eumolpus say that he booked his passage on the ship some time ago, but we realize that he has been forced to this device by his sudden change of plan.

XVIII *Chapters 100–109. Shipboard, Shaven Pates, and a Showdown*

Encolpius is lying on deck trying to sleep. But he is worried by the old poet's penchant for Giton. He tries to reason with himself. All the best things in nature are free; is love an exception? Must it be taken by force and not be received as a gift? The old fellow cannot be a serious rival. He hardly has the stamina to be an effective seducer.

These reflections are shattered by the voices of a man and a woman thirsting for Giton's blood. We are not given any indication of what has prompted this sudden outburst. What can have reminded the indignant pair of Giton? This much we are told, that the man's voice is somehow familiar to Encolpius. We must assume that here is a reminiscence of some incident which has been lost in the abridgement of the *Satyricon,* something which occurred before our heroes arrived in Puteoli. The likeliest explanation of the present situation is that a rendezvous had been fixed between Giton (and possibly Encolpius) and the owners of the voices, who turn out to be the ship's master, Lichas of Tarentum, and a wealthy lady, Tryphaena, also of Tarentum, who spends her time in travel solely for amusement. The rendezvous was perhaps to have been at quayside or actually on board ship. It is clear that neither Encolpius nor Giton had intended to keep the appointment and that it is by pure coincidence that they find themselves in Lichas' ship. Their alarm is evident, so that they must have committed some serious offence in the sight of the offended pair.

The despair of the narrator and his boy is extreme. They pray for death and suspect Eumolpus of betraying them to their enemies. But he disclaims all knowledge of the situation. Lichas is a respectable businessman conveying a cargo to the Tarentum market. Why make him out to be a Cyclops? This is the third reference to the Ulysses story in four chapters. Giton hiding under the bed of the apartment house was twice compared to Homer's hero under the sheep's belly. Can it be that the comparison suggested the idea to our author of switching the setting to a sea voyage? The wanderings of our students are thus compared to the wanderings of Ulysses and his companions, and the wrath of Priapus is a parody of that of Poseidon avenging Polyphemus. A little later on we have a charming Circe to complete the parallel, the whole a burlesque of Greek romance.

Eumolpus is willing to try to help his friends. "Let us imagine," he says, "that we have entered the Cyclops' cave. We must try to escape." A discussion of ways and means follows. It is no good pleading seasickness and to ask to have the boat stop somewhere. The captain would want to see the sufferer. In any case they would be recognized going off the ship. Equally impracticable seems the idea of climbing down a rope into a lifeboat and cutting adrift. No good, says Eumolpus, the night watch would see you, he who spends the night observing the stars.

The resourceful old man offers to wrap them up like bales of luggage and so take them off when they reach port. Encolpius does not think much of that and suggests that they blacken their faces with ink and pass themselves off as Ethiopian slaves. No, says Giton, the ink might come off on our clothing and we should have to curl our hair with tongs, swell out our lips, walk on our heels, and grow beards to make it realistic. Better to throw ourselves overboard and drown.

Finally they decide to shave their heads and eyebrows like runaway slaves and smear a brand mark on their foreheads. Eumolpus' servant, a baker by trade, will do the job. Unfortunately, their preparations are seen by a passenger leaning over the side, troubled with sickness. He curses the horrible sight and staggers back to bed. Depression settles on our gallant band, and they spend a sleepless night.

Petronius has settled down with gusto to the new mise-en-scène, and the Chapters 100–103 are enlivened with delightful comic realism.

Lichas converses with his wealthy and beautiful passenger Tryphaena—the conventional picture of a ship's captain paying court to the most attractive woman on board. He confides to her that Priapus has appeared to him in a dream to reveal that Encolpius for whom he has been searching has been brought on board his ship through the god's agency.

This statement confirms the view that the theme of the *Satyricon* is indeed the wrath of Priapus and that Encolpius is his chief victim. If this is so, then the incident of the violation of the god's rites, referred to in Chapter 16, is a key to the whole narrative and must have occurred not far from the beginning of the original. In which case we have clearly not lost much of the early part of our author's text. The actual violation of the *sacra Priapi* we have lost, if indeed Petronius actually described it, as of course we have lost the incidents which occasioned the resentment of Lichas and Tryphaena.

A second important fact which emerges here is that Lichas, shipowner and captain, businessman and property owner, in short, a solid citizen, enjoys the confidence of Priapus, whose votary we must therefore assume him to be, although a man. Moreover, the god has chosen him to be his agent in inflicting punishment upon Encolpius.

Tryphaena has had a similar nocturnal visitation. Neptune, in the likeness in which she had seen him at Baiae, has told her that she will find Giton in Lichas' ship. Obviously, Neptune has a role corresponding to that of Priapus, to place his victim in the hands of an avenger. Encolpius has offended Priapus, and Giton has offended Neptune. Petronius has combined the Priapus myth with the Ulysses legend. Giton has been compared to Ulysses under the sheep's belly, and Ulysses was pursued by Poseidon (the Greek Neptune). The parallel is not consistently maintained, for it is Encolpius, not Giton, who becomes involved with Circe in Chapters 126 following, and, curiously, Lichas, the champion of Priapus, becomes the victim of Poseidon in Chapter 115 when he is drowned in the shipwreck.

Between Chapters 103 and 104 there is a gap in our present text in which the adventurers must have decided to allow Eumolpus to show himself and renew the acquaintance of Lichas and Tryphaena. In Chapter 104 we find him trying to pour ridicule on their dreams, invoking the rational Epicurus on the subject. Presumably Encolpius and Giton are also present, posing as the poet's slaves.

Lichas has the sailor's superstitious streak and will not ignore the visions vouchsafed to himself and his fair passenger. He is all for searching the ship. This idea suddenly reminds one of the travelers, none other than him who was afflicted with seasickness, of the bizarre scene of head shaving he had witnessed the night before by the light of the moon. He at once recognizes the disguised servants and denounces them and the bad omen of their action, since it is bad luck to cut hair on shipboard unless there is a storm! Petronius again hits at popular superstitions.

Lichas blazes forth at this information and demands the culprits be arraigned before him. Eumolpus bravely admits he gave the order for the shaving so that all should recognize the guilty slaves. "They stole my money," he explains, "and spent it on a mistress they shared between them. I discovered them with her and dragged them away all reeking with perfumes bought at my expense."

Petronius is nicely developing the character of Eumolpus in his new setting. He is no longer merely a hypocritical nuisance, but now displays initiative, courage, and solicitude for his friends.

The captain is adamant that the Guardian Spirit of the ship be placated for the haircutting offense. The culprits are to receive forty stripes apiece. Sailors delegated to the task advance with ropes. Encolpius manfully endures three lashes without flinching. Giton cries out loudly after the first blow. Thereupon Tryphaena recognizes his voice and her serving maids do also. All come running to the rescue. Thus we learn that in an episode now lost to us the boy had spent some time with the lady of Tarentum, long enough to win not only her affections but those of her maids too. His offense is then one of desertion. It is probably fairly recent and occurred just before the arrival in Puteoli. We have already seen something of the boy's fickle nature in his relations with his three male companions.

Meantime Lichas has recognized Encolpius, whose presence he evidently suspects from that of Giton. Coming closer, he confirms his suspicion by an examination of his natural endowments. This may be another hint at the Ulysses legend: the wanderer returning after twenty years and made known to his old nurse by his scar.

Encolpius is acclaimed by Lichas as magnificently furnished with virility. Such was Encolpius' estimate of Ascyltos in Chapter 92. In effect then the two young men are living Priapi. How comes it that they are visited with the god's anger instead of his favor? Is it because of their homosexual behavior which is of course a negation of the function of a fertility god? He has obtained for them their splendid attributes, and they have shown themselves ungrateful by indulging in activities which can in no way be a compliment to their benefactor.

Even Giton cannot escape disfavor. Although gifted with a rather effeminate beauty and fated, as it were, to attract masculine attention of a perverted order, he is after all of the male sex. As we have seen he can easily place his merchandise in the proper quarter, as with Pannychis in Chapter 25, while the protests of Tryphaena and her maids in the present context (105) speak eloquently of the success he has won in their embraces.

We are of course hampered in our speculations by our ignorance of the precise nature of the violation referred to in Chapter 16. In any case, why were Encolpius and his friends press-ganged into the service of reparation which surely should have been conducted by women as their perquisite and in the utmost secrecy? But Petronius has hinted that we must not take the theme seriously. The violation was unintentional and most probably occurred when the youths were taking a short cut through the grotto, the scene of the ritual, on their way from Naples to Puteoli. It is expressly stated in Chapter 16 that Quartilla sought the acquaintance of the offenders more because of their charm than their crime.

In Chapter 106 we learn why Lichas is so angry over Encolpius. He had seduced the captain's wife in the portico of Hercules' temple at Baiae. The place reference suggests that our heroes were at Baiae before coming to Puteoli. We know too from

Tryphaena's dream that Giton's offense also took place at Baiae, probably at Neptune's temple. Lichas is now certain that Priapus and Neptune have acted in concert to place his enemy and Tryphaena's in their power. The lady is won over to his argument that the gods' judgment must be respected and further punishment exacted from the culprits.

Eumolpus now gives an eloquent defense of his friends, showing genuine concern for them. He naturally embraces the opportunity to display his powers as orator as well as poet. He lays stress on the good birth and honesty of his friends and their former ties of friendship with Lichas and Tryphaena.

The speech is a parody of the sort of thing done in the contemporary schools of rhetoric, where absurdly unreal situations were dealt with by equally absurd and unreal arguments. Eumolpus talks of the freeborn status of his friends and then of servile punishments such as of course could not have been applied to free men, whatever their crime. The stigmata which disfigure the faces of Encolpius and Giton are not real and Lichas by now knows this. Yet Eumolpus ignores the point and declares that the victims have willingly branded themselves with ignominy and placed themselves beyond the pale of society. Lichas makes short work of such nonsense and calls the orator to order with a series of pertinent observations. If they came on board of their own free will, why did they shave their heads and change their faces to avoid recognition? Why did you, their advocate, attempt to conceal them? You say they were our friends; on this account they deserve even severer treatment.

"You are full of ill will," says Eumolpus. "These people only wanted to tidy themselves up by having their hair cut short." "Since when," retorts the other, "does a shaven pate attract sympathy?"

The chapter is a delightful satire, kept within reasonable bounds, since such high-flown verbosity was all too familiar to Petronius' readers in everyday experience. They themselves had had to sweat through this kind of exercise as part of their education.

Encolpius for his part is terrified. At the same time, brought back into the world of common sense by the captain's harshly sane reasoning, he realizes how ridiculous he looks with shaven head and eyebrows and ink-stained features, how unfit to plead his case. But, alas, when his face is washed for him, Lichas' fury is increased, as he recognizes more clearly the seducer of his wife.

Things are going from bad to worse, and now it will come to blows. Eumolpus has his valet and one or two passengers will take his side, duly armed with the razors which the poet's man still carries in stock. The adversaries advance to the fray, and there are casualties.

Swiftly the action turns to melodramatic farce. Giton threatens to mutilate himself in that part of his anatomy dearest to his admirers. Tryphaena at once intervenes to prevent this catastrophe, and at the instigation of the pilot who acts as peacemaker, she consents to initiate proceedings for a truce. Borrowing an olive branch from the image of the ship's Guardian Spirit, she launches into epic hexameters. At once the fighting spirit of the combatants is deflated. Perhaps they have never met a woman poet before. She is obviously something straight out of mime, like the rest of the scene just enacted.

Eumolpus seizes the opportunity to display his talents as a lawyer and draws up a treaty with the proper phraseology and the penalties for violation duly laid down.

The amazing thing about this piece of legal virtuosity is that it puts all the blame upon Lichas and Tryphaena. They are bound by the strictest terms not to take any further measures against Encolpius and Giton or to visit them with any unwelcome attentions. Not a word is said about the young pair's misdemeanors which occasioned the wrath of their opponents, whose capitulation seems utterly unexpected and unreal, especially as there is no indication that they were worsted in the conflict so abruptly broken off.

Only one explanation is possible in logic, if we care to give it, knowing of course that the whole thing is a burlesque. Petronius' verisimilitude lies in the details of his exposition, never in the narrative itself. The truth then is that Tryphaena is so enamored of the attractive boy that she will do anything to regain his favors. Lichas too is overcome by Encolpius' weighty charms. What now of Priapus and Neptune? Their cause seems to have suffered eclipse. But, as we shall shortly see, the slighted divinities are not prepared to let matters rest thus.

XIX *Chapters 109–112. Merriment and a Milesian Tale*

To celebrate the peace treaty a feast is prepared, and a sudden calm of the ocean ensues, which, under the circumstances, ought to make the hilarious diners pause to reflect. But those whom the gods wish to destroy—. Some of the passengers indulge in a little fishing as a contribution to the festive fare, while others catch birds on limed sticks. Petronius conjures up for us an exquisite little picture of the victims' feathers floating in the air and settling on the water to twist and turn with its slight movement. The whole work is full of such imagery. For the critic to analyze it and even to attempt to describe it is to destroy its magic. The easy grace of the Arbiter's style is inimitable.

Eumolpus has by now really come into his own. He dominates the scene, secure in his reputation as a skillful advocate and negotiator. He has certainly gained in stature since Petronius decided to jettison the vague Ascyltos in favor of developing his more colorful substitute. He remains nonetheless a rogue and a ponderous and pretentious humbug in the true picaresque style.

His irrepressible bent for versification again asserts itself, under the stimulus of wine. He proceeds to make disparaging remarks in mime tradition against the shaven and stigmatized pair, then laments the departure of their fallen locks first in elegiacs and then in hendecasyllabics.

A serving girl of Tryphaena's, moved by this dirge, seeks to repair the damage by providing the unfortunates with wigs and false eyebrows from her mistress' wardrobe, completely restoring them in the eyes of the lady and the captain. Whereupon our poet is moved to witticisms at the expense of fickle womanhood and reminded of a story which, he says, is a true one and took place within his own time.

We are accordingly regaled with our second Milesian tale, the most famous and delightful of all the anecdotes in Petronius. It is this more than any other which made his reputation in the centuries to come and was known to many scholars in the Dark Ages, long before the Banquet of Trimalchio was rediscovered.

Clearly Eumolpus, always eager to express himself in public regardless of the consequences, is loth to relinquish the hegemony he has recently acquired. At long last he has found an appreciative audience, and he resolves to make the most of the situation.

In this he succeeds magnificently, thanks to the wonderful story of the Matron of Ephesus which his creator has kept back until now for this moment of glory for the browbeaten beggar poet. As with the Pergamene Boy (Chapters 85–87), so now with the Ephesian Matron (Chapters 111–112), Eumolpus reveals that his true métier is not that of poet, rhetorician, lawyer, or resourceful rogue, although for better or for worse he is all of these things when occasion demands or our resistance is lowered, but rather of inspired raconteur. Here is no bombast, no repetition of detail, no superfluous rhetoric, but a simple, straightforward narrative, with grace and charm, economy and vivacity of language. In verse Eumolpus is turgid and inane; in prose a consummate artist.

Petronius is at his best in telling of the foibles and eccentricities of women. Catullus and Ovid are not more versed in their wiles or more witty in exposing them. But the same good humor is evident in his treatment of them as of his male characters. This does not necessarily mean that he approved of them. At the court of Nero he lived close to some of the most repellent specimens of the fair sex that history tells of. The even temper of our author is a mark of that mental discipline he was able to assume, the moral courage which was his defense in life. Given the circumstances of his chosen mode of existence, its essential escapism, we know that the light-heartedness of his writing was assumed, not genuine. Nowhere I think does the fact more clearly reveal itself than in the completely amoral tale he now proceeds to tell with cynical detachment, entrusting its telling to a deceitful, unscrupulous, and rather obscene old man whose character it admirably suits. Petronius warns us not to condemn, not to attempt to shatter the armor of defense.

The matron of Ephesus, says Eumolpus, was of such outstanding virtue that women from neighboring communities felt impelled to come and gaze upon such a marvel. Could it have been that she was a little complacent at this state of affairs?

It is otiose to enquire into a possible local origin of the story. Petronius may have picked up the Milesian version in Asia Minor, but the matron is not simply of Ephesus or of Miletus, or of India or China before that. She is universal, and the situation in which she finds herself is a commonplace of human experience. Women of irreproachable conduct often lose their husbands by death or some other form of desertion. Such is the ingratitude of human nature that the husbands do not continue to live with their paragons but find escape in death from a partnership for which they feel themselves unworthy. Perhaps it is Nature's law of the survival of the fittest. Petronius' irony is brought out in the first sentence which in the Latin literally means "she invited them to the spectacle of herself." It was to a kind of sideshow that holiday makers came from the districts surrounding Ephesus to see the "world's most virtuous wife."

Therefore (*ergo*), says our author, having conveyed her husband forth for burial—the words imply that he died of her chastity—she was not content merely to follow the coffin with disheveled hair and beating her bared bosom, but proceeded to follow him into the burial vault and to install herself therein to watch over the corpse and to weep by night and day until death should claim her also. Her parents and relatives could not dissuade her from pursuing her dreadful resolve, which she sought to hasten by refusing food and drink. The mayor and leading citizens also come to plead with her, only to be repulsed and to depart.

Five days passed thus, while a faithful maidservant stayed behind in the vault, adding her tears to those of her mistress and renewing from time to time the supply of oil to keep the lamp burning, so that they could see their tears and the object of them. No doubt the lamp was also a help to would-be spectators of this exemplary grief, for, says Petronius, people of all ranks of life were united in agreement that here shone forth a unique example of true love and chastity.

Now it so happened that the governor of the province, whose headquarters were at Ephesus, had ordered the crucifixion of some thieves. This now took place close beside the vault in which the lady was bewailing her loss. A soldier was placed on guard to prevent the bodies of the criminals being carried off for burial before they had served their purpose of salutary admonition to passers-by. He saw the light burning and heard the widow's groans.

His idle curiosity was roused, for such is defective human nature, says our author. Descending into the vault, he perceived a most beautiful woman. We had not been told that she was beautiful as well as good, but of course we had guessed it. He was naturally taken aback at what he imagined to be an apparition from the infernal regions. Then, seeing the corpse and the woman's tearful face, lacerated by her fingernails in the paroxysms of grief, he decided that she could not support the loss of her husband. It was his obvious duty to try to console her. Accordingly, he decamped into the tomb. "We all have to come to the same end and find the same resting place," said he among similar conventional words of condolence. The widow, however, redoubled her expressions of grief, tearing her hair and depositing handfuls of it upon the coffin.

The soldier tries to persuade the widow and her maid to eat and drink. The maid submits, overcome by the fumes of the wine. She joins her exhortations to live to those of the soldier, quoting a line of Virgil in support of her arguments. The mistress is overcome by Virgil, as the maid by the wine, and allows herself to eat with a good appetite.

After this not too hard-won victory, the soldier now attempts to assail a virtue whose international fame he is perhaps not aware of. It so happens that he is handsome and can plead his cause with eloquence, so much so that he finds favor in the eyes of the love-starved widow. The maid obligingly seconds him with more pleading borrowed from Anna's advice to Dido in Book Four of the *Aeneid.*

For the next two or three days, visitors to the tomb found the doors shut, so that they must have concluded that the poor widow had expired of grief. Such, however, was not the case. The woman was simply making up for lost time in the arms of one who was able to show her that life was well worth living. The pair in fact set up house in their rather unusual quarters, and the new husband sets forth by day to do the shopping, returning at nightfall to the love nest and domestic bliss.

Fate is unkind. For one day, finding the place of crucifixion unguarded, relatives of one of the victims remove the body and commit it to burial. The soldier, discerning the loss, is fearful of punishment and confides in the widow. He will have to put himself to the sword to atone for his neglect. The widow feels that two deaths of nearest and dearest are more than she could bear. With instant resolution, expressed with epigrammatic precision and directness, she solves the problem. "I prefer," says she, "to sacrifice a dead man than to kill off a live one." She orders her husband's body to be removed from its coffin and to be affixed to the vacant cross. No time is wasted over making use of the intelligent woman's stratagem, and next day passers-by wonder how the defunct husband has arrived in his new position.

This perfect example of the art of the raconteur is vouched for by Eumolpus as belonging to his own time. Perhaps we are to assume that it came to his knowledge while on service in the province of Asia, of which Ephesus was in effect the chief city and residence of the governor. Miletus, which gave its name to the genre, was also in this province, as was Pergamum, the setting of Eumolpus' other tale. He is in fact the hero, if such we may call him, of the seduction of the Pergamene Boy which occurred while Eumolpus was a soldier in the retinue of the quaestor and stationed in the city. All of which does suggest that both tales were picked up by our author when he himself was on service in the East, probably on the occasion of his governorship of nearby Bithynia. We may therefore reasonably assume that the *Satyricon* was composed after his return to Rome in A.D. 61.

The telling of such tales is then, as we have already remarked, the true vocation of Eumolpus. If only he would confine himself to it! Petronius has put two superb examples into his mouth to prove the point, and he has acquitted himself in masterly fashion on both occasions. Circumstances have made of him a rhetorician and versifier, and in both capacities he earns nothing but ridicule and abuse. Thus does the Arbiter condemn the prevailing fashion of the day. Art for art's sake must fail unless practiced by an artist of genius. How much better for a man of the people to exercise his talents in the field of storytelling for which Nature has fitted him. The age of Petronius has worked to death the legacy of the Republican period, the epic poem and the elegiac, the formal speech, the philosophic discussion. It is time to look further afield for inspiration. A whole new world awaits exploration in the folk tale, the oral tradition of the vagrant entertainer, enriched with his accumulation of experience in travel, his contact with many lands and peoples. Here is something new for the *satyricos* to study and propagate, to bring to the rich man's table and to the literary salon.

Eumolpus the humbug, the shady opportunist, the sly-witted plebeian is worth cultivating. He speaks for the common man. He and Trimalchio and all they represent are worth more than the futile Encolpius and Ascyltos whose shallow training in Agamemnon's school has given them ideas above their station. Eumolpus has received similar training in youth, and it has done him signal disservice, but life has taught him better accomplishments. Perhaps it will teach the young men in their turn. Meantime, Eumolpus is at home in the *Satyricon* and they are not. He would have graced Trimalchio's feast; they can only sit silent and shudder.

XX *Chapters 113–115. Storm and Shipwreck*

The sailors enjoy the story as well they might. Tryphaena, on the other hand, and here we see once more Petronius' skill in the portrayal of character, is suffused with blushes, recognizing in the Matron a fellow victim of Venus' wiles. Lichas is made of sterner stuff; the governor should have put the husband's body back in the tomb and crucified the widow. He is thinking of the infidelity of his own wife, another weak woman. As for Encolpius, he is discontented. The new treaty imposes restraint on him also, the ex-favorite of Lichas, now only too secure from his attentions. To cap it all, Tryphaena is slobbering all over Giton who won't speak to him any more.

Priapus seems then to be tormenting Encolpius again. One of Tryphaena's maids seeks to console him, advising him not to pay any more attention to her mistress than to a prostitute. But the youth is still worried. He even fears that the jester in Eumolpus will again come to the fore and that the dirty old man will make fun of him in more of his dreadful verse.

The truce lately concluded has after all been a defiance of Priapus and Neptune who had contrived to bring the guilty parties on ship where justice should have been executed upon them. And now they reveal their displeasure at the thwarting of their design. Dark clouds descend and envelop the ship. Diverse winds blow, and the vessel is driven this way and that. Lichas implores Encolpius to restore the sacred veil and rattle (*sistrum*) of Isis which apparently he stole from the ship in some episode now lost to us. Isis, an Egyptian divinity, had, by Hellenistic times, acquired attributes in common with Venus, and no doubt the possession of her magic symbols had enabled Encolpius to put the captain's wife, whose name we now learn was Hedyle, into his power of seduction.

At this point, Neptune, fearing perhaps that Isis, if her powers are restored to her, may thwart his plan anew, sweeps Lichas into the sea where he is sucked under by the swirling waters. Tryphaena too is near to death, but her servants seize her and place her with her luggage in the lifeboat. Encolpius and Giton resolve to die in each other's arms, and to facilitate this, they tie themselves together, finding consolation that they will thus be united in death. Meanwhile, the ship is smashed to pieces, for such is the will of the offended gods. Some fishermen approach the wreck to pillage it, but seeing the survivors they come to their rescue.

Follows the culmination of the absurd. In the midst of this melodramatic situation, a burlesque of Greek romance but also reminiscent of the farfetched themes of the school of declamation, Eumolpus is discovered below deck engaged upon an epic. Apparently the debacle has inspired him. Another hit at the extravagant subject matter of contemporary poetry. His friends overpower him and drag him unwilling to safety.

The survivors pass a restless night in a fisherman's cabin. On the morrow they find Lichas' corpse washed up on the shore. Encolpius is overcome with emotion at the sight and delivers a piece of rhetoric which would surely win him a prize in Agamemnon's classroom. Then the body is burnt, and of course Eumolpus composes an epitaph.

XXI *Chapters 116–125. A Project for Mime and a Slice of Epic*

Thus ends the ship episode. We now come to the final section of the *Satyricon,* the adventures of Encolpius, Giton, and Eumolpus at Croton, on the tip of Italy.

The little party makes its way from the seashore inland and, climbing a hill, they see before them the city, perched also on a height. A countryman informs them that it is Croton, and they are excited at the prospect of visiting this most ancient city, at one time the largest in Italy, now fallen into decline after disastrous wars.

At last it seems that Fortune is to smile upon our wanderers. Croton, the countryman tells them, is no longer a place for the businessman, but if anyone has some pretense to quick-wittedness and can tell lies the whole day long, then he has found a gold mine in this fair city.

Petronius uses for quick-witted the word *urbanus.* It occurs frequently throughout the *Satyricon,* denoting the smartness and hypocrisy which its literal meaning, "belonging to a city," "city-bred," has come to convey. *Urbanus* and *urbanitas* in their best sense imply good breeding, refinement, and education, but more often in Latin literature they imply the sharpness of mind which city life instills and with it opportunism and unscrupulousness. The term *urbanus* is often applied to the parasite and flatterer, as for example in Plautus and Terence, and to the jester, whether professional or amateur, the so-called *scurra* whom we meet so often in the Roman authors.[10] Eumolpus has much in common with the *scurra,* not as poet or raconteur, but as satirist and cynic and, not least, as the improviser of deceit for whom the situation which now presents itself is a godsend.

For Croton has degenerated through its poverty into a city of fortune hunters. No one marries there, no one has heirs, for to do so is to be outlawed from society. Only the childless are esteemed, for they have something to leave—to others.

Petronius satirizes in Croton a state of affairs all too common in Rome and takes the opportunity to denounce a plague of his time, the fortune hunter, whose unwelcome attentions he undoubtedly suffered himself as a man of wealth and probably unmarried and childless. His cultured, fastidious temperament must have particularly loathed this particular form of social vulture. It is yet another aspect of that hypocrisy which is a recurrent theme of his work. Few of his characters are exempt from the vice. Trimalchio is perhaps the exception. He is vulgar and ostentatious but withal honest. But he no longer needs to practice deceit and flattery. Yet to arrive at his present wealth and power, he must have practiced these things to no small degree. In short, no one escapes reproach.

The *Satyricon* is not primarily a work of satire. But Petronius' good-natured tolerance breaks down at times, and we sense the bitterness behind the mockery when hypocrisy raises her Medusa's head.

How vivid is the picture conjured up by the countryman's parting words to the strangers (end of Chapter 116)—"You are approaching a city which resembles a landscape ravaged by the plague, where one may see only corpses being torn to pieces and the ravens which are tearing them." The picture in our author's mind is not merely Croton but Rome and the whole Roman world.

Eumolpus reflects upon this situation and declares himself not displeased at the turn of events. The artist in him is awakened, and he expresses himself in the language of the Theater Arts—the language of the *Satyricos*. "If only," he says, "I had a more ample backcloth, more appropriate costumes, a more attractive set of props, I could then put across this piece of deception without delay and lead you all on to fame and fortune."

Here then speaks the master showman, eminently qualified by temperament and training in the schools of rhetoric and of experience to play the leading role in a real-life drama of deceit and imposture. It is the chance of a lifetime which will compensate for the lean years of infamy and abuse. Hypocrisy is vindicated at last, sneers Petronius.

"Let us then put together our play, and put me in charge if the idea of doing business attracts you." An oath of loyalty to Eumolpus is made, like that of gladiators to their manager, binding them to his service body and soul. The word used for play in this context is *mimus*, and the events about to be described are obviously of the kind which furnish material for popular farce. "The Legacy Hunters" would be an ideal title for this sort of thing. The theme of deception is common to the *fabulae palliatae*, adapted from the Greek New Comedy, but the highly farcical and indecent incidents involving Circe and Priapic remedial rites do not belong to the middle-class comedy background of the *palliatae*. Mime is much more in the satyric vogue of the first century A.D. Women, we may recall, performed in the mime, and it is hard to imagine the charming Circe being played by a male actor, as she would have to be in a *palliata*.

The plot devised by Eumolpus is thus: he is to play the part of a rich man who has lost his only son, a young man of brilliant promise. The old man has left his native city to avoid the scene of his bereavement and to escape the attentions of interested clients. A recent disaster at sea had added to his misfortune, with the shipwreck of twenty millions worth of merchandise. The loss itself means little to him, so wealthy is he, but all the same he has suffered some diminution of status.

There still remain to him vast estates in Africa, in Numidia to be precise, with thousands of slaves, enough to capture Carthage so to speak, property and investments worth say thirty millions. We are reminded of Trimalchio, and we must not forget that our author too had wealth of this scale, a piquant detail that his listeners would appreciate as he read them this passage of his burlesque.

Excellent so far. Just a few more details, advise the troupers, to really whet the appetites of the Crotonians. The old boy must cultivate a troublesome cough, complain of stomach disorders, and refuse his food. He must talk all the time about his gold and show greed in the collection of his revenues, grumbling that his lands don't yield enough. Let him spend his days working out his accounts and keep on about making a new will.

Eumolpus and Encolpius are eager to put their scheme into effect and hasten on towards the city with such speed that poor Giton, helping to carry their baggage, falters in his too often assumed role of slave, while Corax the barber, Eumolpus' hired man, talks of dumping his load and taking to his heels. Thus they would remind their masters that their services are valuable and will merit in due course a share of the profits.

To relieve the tension caused by the threat of mutiny, Eumolpus gives an exposé of the art of writing epics. We are not to suppose that the sudden change in his fortunes has changed his (mistaken) conception of his real vocation. A nice bit of psychological insight on Petronius' part. The old incorrigible is too thick-skinned to be capable of self-criticism. His self-confidence increased, he is more than ever convinced of his poetic genius. And so he proceeds to explain that for the writing of epics, more than mere ideas and the urge to relax from practical affairs are needed. One must have a solid foundation of experience based on the study of the best models and a full command of the *style noble* which avoids all vulgarisms. He cites the authority of Horace's "I loathe the profane mob and keep them at a distance" (*Odes*, 3.1.1). Homer, the Greek lyric poets, Roman Virgil, and Horace with his painstaking felicity, these are the sole guides for the true art.

To illustrate his remarks, Eumolpus chooses the theme currently in vogue of the Civil War, an immense subject requiring a complete possession of one's letters. Furthermore, the work must not be a mere compilation of historical facts—leave that to the historians; throughout the whole complicated mass of divine interventions and the convolutions of thought and imagery the poet's prophetic inspiration must shine, rather than a mere scrupulous adherence to the sources of his material.

With this injunction, our underestimated bard now treats his subdued companions to two hundred and ninety-five hexameters.

He begins with a long tirade against the luxury and vice of

Rome, mistress of the world, her greed for new riches and pleasures, and the demoralization they bring. This is a favorite subject with the impoverished poet and his present language reminds us of his similar denunciations of wealth in Chapters 84 and 88. Whatever territory is prosperous is treated as an enemy, so that its riches may be plundered. The victorious Roman soldiers bring back treasures from the East, Corinthian bronze, gold ornaments, and garments dyed with Tyrian purple. These new objects of delight make them lose interest in the simple pleasures of life. They take joy in the adoption of effeminate Eastern practices, eunuchs and pretty boys, exotic dress, rare articles of food and drink. Worst of all is the craze for bringing back hordes of savage animals to fight in the arena and to be gorged with human blood. Magistracies are purchased by popular entertainment, the Senate itself is corrupted by gold. Even the older citizens have forgotten the virtues of their Republican youth.

In Chapter 120, at Verse 67 of the poem in question, there is an interesting allusion to an underground locality, a kind of entrance to the infernal regions, situated between Parthenope (the ancient name for Naples) and Dicarchis (Puteoli). It is described as lying in a steep declivity, bathed by the waters of the underworld river Cocytos, a place of noxious exhalations and foul humidity. Pluto, the god of these regions, here addresses Fortuna, and she promises him upheavals for a too-complacent Rome.

This place, divested of its mythology, is none other than the grotto (*crypta*) mentioned in Chapter 16 as the scene of Quartilla's nocturnal revelry. Petronius must have known the spot as it was close to his own estates at Cumae, and his imagination, stirred by the place and its legends, leads him to introduce it here.

The insertion of this personal reminiscence induces me to suppose that these verses put into Eumolpus' mouth are simply Petronius' own humorous parody of the bombast of his age, composed purely as an entertainment, without any particular desire to satirize Lucan's epic on the Civil War. It is true that the latter work, at least the first book, had recently made its debut, but, as I have said, the theme was a popular one, as was also the capture of Troy, Nero's favorite, a version of which Eumolpus gave us in Chapter 89. There must have been many such contributions composed at the time. The present examples have survived simply because they were inserted in the *Satyricon*. Certainly the treatment of the theme is satirical, but not of a personal nature, for there is no evidence of an attack upon individuals in Petronius' work. The whole thing is simply an example of the "immense volubility" (*ingens volubilitas verborum* is the phase employed in Chapter 124) of Eumolpus and the schools of rhetoric.

The flow of eloquence is sufficient to cover the journey to the gates of Croton. The party is soon made welcome, once the news is spread according to plan. As foreseen, the fortune-hunting Crotonians, on learning of Eumolpus' reputed wealth, vie with each other in loading him with attentions and gifts.

Apparently Dame Fortune is disposed to be kind, for the time being at any rate. Things are going extremely well, we are told at the beginning of Chapter 125. A lacuna preceding it suggests that the epitomist thought it better to omit the details. Eumolpus is jubilant, forgetting the past injustices of the hostile goddess. But Encolpius, with his usual pessimism, is not so sure that this wave of prosperity will last. Supposing someone were to send to Africa to investigate Eumolpus' territorial pretensions? What if Corax should turn traitor? He is weary of this continuous existence outside the law, a significant remark from our wandering scholar!

From this point almost to the end of our fragments we are again among the ladies, in circumstances not dissimilar to those narrated in the early part of the work. Petronius follows the practice of classical drama in allotting importance to the role of lady's maid, a convention also followed, be it noted, in the Milesian tale of the Matron of Ephesus. So here, in these present chapters (126 following) we have the *ancilla* Chrysis who is active in her mistress' affairs, like Psyche in those of Quartilla (16 following). Both Circe and Quartilla are mainly concerned, like all the women of the *Satyricon*, with lovemaking, as votaries of Venus or more particularly of her son Priapus.

There is then an interesting parallel between the beginning and the end of the fragments, both of which consist of more or less serious literary discussion followed by adventures of a licentious and farcical nature over which a vengeful Priapus presides. Chapters 1–4 are a discussion of oratory with illustrative verses in Chapter 5. Then follow the incidents leading to involvement with Quartilla (6–15) and the actual involvement (16–26). Similarly, towards the end of the work, we have a discussion of poetry (118) illustrated by the slice of epic (119–124), leading up to the adventure with Circe (126–139).

Thus we seem to have completed a circle, which would argue for an imminent completion of the whole work, an impression heightened by the fact that, as we shall shortly see, Mercury, the god of business and opportunism as well as patron of scholars and travelers, intervenes in the shape of a cash offering to rescue Encolpius from his ordeal with the Priapic priestess Oenothea, so that very shortly afterwards he is able to make his escape.

It is true that the narrative does start up again, after what might seem to be its logical conclusion, continuing for another three chapters, now in a very mutilated condition, and coming to an abrupt end in our fragments. We must remember that the *Satyricon* is a serial story. No doubt an enthusiastic admirer urged our author to continue beyond the Priapic cycle at least to tell us more of Eumolpus' adventures with the Crotonians. It looks as though with this episode Petronius took on more than he had bargained for, and it is difficult to see how Eumolpus' imposture could end otherwise than in a disastrous exposure, throwing its inventor and his companions back into their impecunious and vagrant condition.

XXII *Chapters 126–141 (end). Priapus versus Mercury*

Chrysis, Circe's maid, is an interesting study. She thinks that she is better than her mistress and has more discriminating tastes. This is another conventional trait in a conventional character. She admires Encolpius and guesses that he is something more than he makes himself out to be. He is passing himself off as a slave but has elegant ways which belie this station. For herself, Chrysis prefers men of substance, knights for example, the sort of people who get the best seats reserved for them in the theater. Her mistress, however, is like many women of rank: she favors men of the lower orders like slaves and gladiators, jumping over the rows of equestrian stalls, as it were, into the back of the pit to find her amours. Is Petronius here thinking of some of the highborn ladies of his acquaintance?

There is a lacuna preceding this chapter (126) and we are not told how Encolpius, who in his present role bears the name Polyaenos, which is none other than that given by the sirens to Ulysses (Homer, *Odyssey*, 12, 184), has met up with Chrysis, but we learn that he is now made up fit to kill, with his hair in curls, his cheeks adorned with cosmetics, that he has a languorous look doubtless helped along with eye shadow and affects a mincing step and a swaying motion full of invitation.

The ambitious maid, however, will have none of him, and so he asks her to arrange a meeting for him with her mistress in a nearby grove of plane trees. Agreed. Chrysis departs, reappearing after a short interval with the lady in question, who apparently had been waiting hidden all the time in hopes of the rendezvous. We may in fact conjecture that Encolpius has been invited to the spot by the promise of a secret tryst.

And now for the first time in the *Satyricon* we are introduced to a woman of outstanding beauty and charm. Impossible to do justice to her, says Encolpius, trying hard. Long natural curls spread right over her shoulders, a narrow forehead (a mark of beauty for the Greco-Roman mind) from which the hair sprang up vigorously, curving eyebrows running from the line of her cheeks almost to meet in the space between her eyes, eyes brighter than the stars on a moonless night, gently curving nostrils and a mouth, the incarnation of a kiss, such as Praxiteles carved for Diana. Chin, throat, and hands whiter than Parian marble, as also her feet imprisoned in the gold threads of her sandals. Thus appeared the delicious Circe, worthy namesake of Homer's sorceress, daughter of the Sun. So fair is she that for the first time in his life Encolpius can forget Doris, his earliest love! Promptly he breaks into verse which, as we have seen, he only does in moments of strong emotion. He is astonished that Jupiter can sit there idle in Heaven—here is the real Danae.[11] To win her he should at once disguise himself and come down on Earth.

This charming tribute delights Circe. She offers him her love, but newly awakened this very year. True, Encolpius already has a fraternal love in Giton, but she will offer him a sister's solace to complete his happiness. It is the will of the gods. She is Circe, he is Polyaenos. These two legendary names must spell a great passion.

Encolpius is more than willing but, alas, Priapus intervenes to put a curse upon his virility, and disastrous failure ensues. His lovely partner is insulted and distressed. Frantically she appeals to Chrysis and to her mirror. What has befallen her charms, how has she failed to please? Encolpius too is horror stricken as though awakening from some nightmare. His forebodings in Chapter 125 are being realized, though not in the way he had expected. He had feared a return to poverty, not a sudden, presumably never before experienced, loss of his personal powers. This is a far greater tragedy, to be deprived of the means by which he has hitherto earned his keep. He will have to resort to his brains, a fate successfully avoided until now. He is even estranged from Giton and for the same sad reason.

The humiliation is not over. For Circe's letter delivered by Chrysis is penned with acid contempt. Chrysis has a soft spot for Encolpius and consoles him. Such things are not uncommon at Croton where witchcraft is practiced. A remedy shall be provided for the youth's defective powers. Here is another echo of the Quartilla episode, when a remedy had to be provided for the violation of Priapus' rites.

Encolpius writes to apologize to Circe. He declares that he does not know who or what is responsible for his default. The letter is short, in crisp, vigorous sentences showing a businesslike resolve to make amends. It is the dignified *mea culpa* of one who is not used to defeat and who is confident that it will not occur again. He takes vigorous measures of self-discipline, careful diet and—to bed without Giton.

Next morning, our hero betakes himself to the trysting place beneath the plane trees. Chrysis in due course appears, but not with Circe. Indeed, an old woman accompanies her to practice ritual magic on the offender. Success seems assured. Petronius once more satirizes the grotesque applications of popular superstition.

The plane grove is an idyllic setting for lovers' dalliance. Circe tries her luck once more. All goes well at first but then again disaster. The fair lady is furious. Encolpius is spat upon and reviled, the slaves including Chrysis get a beating. Thoroughly ashamed, Encolpius takes refuge in his room and attempts to mutilate himself. He finds this impossible for there is nothing left to mutilate! He addresses the offender with bitter reproach and three lines from Virgil.

Petronius takes the opportunity, after this somewhat indecent passage of comical rage, to defend his work in verses which recall those of Martial and Ovid when vindicating their outspoken writings. (Chapter 132 and see Martial, *Epigrams,* XI, 2; Ovid, *Remedia Amoris,* 316 f.). We have already referred to them and to the famous phrase "a work of refreshing candor" (*novae simplicitatis opus*), the term with which the author characterizes his straightforward account, in plain but graceful language, of the doings of ordinary folk. In this little poem the whole purpose of the *Satyricon* is resumed. It is the most effective blow at pretension and hypocrisy, whether of thought or of language, that could be devised, revealing at the same time the author's own attitude towards these curses of his day.

There follows a prayer in seventeen hexameters to Priapus at a shrine of his, presumably in Croton. Encolpius realizes, as Chrysis could not, that his loss of virility was due to the god and not to the witches of the locality. He promises a goat and a pig if his fortunes are restored, with flowing wine and young people to dance round the shrine. Priapus is invoked as companion of the Nymphs and of Bacchus, whose son he is by Dione (Venus), and as a woodland spirit, like Pan and the Satyrs. Thus we see that his place in the *Satyricon* is natural and fitting, although malignant.

A hideous old woman, by name Proselenos, who, it appears, is an attendant of the local priestess of Priapus, Oenothea, seizes Encolpius at his supplications and drags him to the priestess' abode belaboring him with her broomstick. Oenothea arrives and, learning of the young man's deficiency, promises to put matters right.

The propitiation ceremony is of a curiously homely kind and begins with preparations for a meal of pork and beans. Encolpius is put to work to shell the latter, and, while so engaged, he describes in another spate of hexameters the humble interior of the priestess' kitchen.

Various comic details enliven Petronius' satire on the decrepit and sordid milieu which is to witness the atonement. But deliverance is at hand. Left alone for a moment Encolpius goes to the kitchen door. Three geese advance upon him, hoping to be fed and, disappointed, attack him. One of them he manages to kill with a leg which he breaks off the table. But the geese are sacred to Priapus. Poor Encolpius is now in still greater trouble. In despair, he offers the priestess two pieces of gold as compensation for her loss. The effect is instantaneous. Encolpius is forgiven. Mercury has intervened to save his protégé.

There follow the famous verses, so often quoted by admirers of the *Satyricon* through the centuries, beginning "Whoever has money shall always sail with a favoring wind and control fortune at his will" (137.9). They are the ultimate moral of the book. Not even a fertility god can prevail against the god of commerce.

This little incident of the bribing of a priestess, whose religious fervor is brought to nothing by the glint of gold, while making the conventional point that wanderers and students are protected by Mercury, at the same time stresses, in the interests of satire, that greed and hypocrisy are the prevailing and universal characteristics of mankind, the constant theme of Petronius' work, although lightly handled and with indulgence. And it is of course Rome's greed which purchases for her the things of the East, including the wretched Easterners themselves who flock to Italy, bringing their ridiculous and obscene religions with them.

Encolpius escapes, and there is some indication that his powers are returning, although he expresses doubt and pessimism in still more verse (139). But Chrysis pursues him ardently and he seems to be able to please her. The text is mutilated, no doubt in the interests of our modesty. Chapter 140 however, hardly suitable reading for schoolgirls, has largely been preserved, probably because of the exquisite irony of Petronius' style. It is now Eumolpus' turn to be favored by Priapus who must have a liking for the old poet on account of his prowess in the past.

A matron named Philomela, who in her youth had extorted many an inheritance but is now bereft of the charms necessary for such work, offers to Eumolpus the services of her son and daughter who are evidently being trained to carry on the family business. A salacious scene follows in which Petronius' wicked humor surpasses itself, and the episode has a strongly Milesian flavor. Our poet chooses the girl, Encolpius the boy. At first Priapus' mean spirit is still abroad, but eventually Mercury intervenes once and for all, with a decisiveness which compels the admiration of the old poet.

After several gaps in the text we come to the final chapter (141). It seems that the legacy hunters are getting impatient for some sight of Eumolpus' riches. The time has come to offer them a share in his will. But the old man makes a curious stipulation. His beneficiaries may only enter into possession of their legacies if they consent to cut up his body and devour the pieces in public. It is the custom among certain peoples, he tells them, for the dead to be eaten by their relatives.

We can only guess what device our mime producers have hit upon. No doubt they would substitute some corpse or a dummy disguised as Eumolpus while they made a last-minute getaway. We leave them at the point where a Crotonian named Gorgias is on the point of complying, encouraged by a voice which would appear to be that of Eumolpus!

This final twist seems to be a desperate one. It looks as though Petronius has grown weary of his narrative and hardly knows what to think up next. If so, this last chapter of our fragments cannot be far removed from what was effectually the end of the original compilation.

CHAPTER 4

The Influence of Petronius

THE Petronius story is fraught with irony and paradox. It would seem that apart from his own day, when presumably a select audience at Nero's court accorded a warm welcome to his recital of the doings of lesser mortals, our author has been best understood by a mere handful of scholars at a time of official disapproval. On the other hand, in recent years, through the media of novel and cinema, Petronius has been a familiar figure in the imagination of thousands who have never read his work or even heard of it.

In Petronius we are confronted with three distinct entities—the man, the courtier, and the artist. We have seen that the Arbiter was an individualist with a highly personal mode of existence. His fastidious and critical spirit prevented him from being in any way a typical satellite of Nero; hence his attraction for the youthful emperor, himself a man of undoubted talent and originality who would have continued to enjoy the older man's civilizing influence, had his natural weakness not predisposed him to submit to baser examples of conduct.

But neither as a personality nor as a member of the imperial entourage is our author clearly revealed in the *Satyricon*. Precisely because of this, some element of doubt persists even today as to the authorship and date of the work. One thing is certain; it is unique in literature, the creation of a most original mind which deliberately refrains from putting a personal stamp upon it. By instinct rather do we feel that Tacitus' Petronius must be the author. We have no proof of the connection.

Its unique character forbids us to assign the work to any single category of literature. In my second chapter, I have considered the *Satyricon* as an amalgam and suggested the genres to which it seems to me[1] to be indebted. But the work is no mere hotchpotch. Even in its present truncated form it has homogeneity, the whole constituting as it were a new genre to which we may rightly assign the name satyric, reflected in the traditional title of *Satyricon* —an *opus satyricum.*

The title is traditional, but it has puzzled the understanding of admirers and critics through the centuries. Add to this that few ages have possessed the work in anything but scattered fragments until the seventeenth century. This or that particle was held by this or that scholar for his individual enjoyment and assessment. Hence a variety of appreciations and attitudes have arisen across time, highly subjective or conditioned by prevailing thought and national temperament.

The general nature of Petronius' influence is the sum of varying reactions to distinct sections of his work, now the moral *dicta,* now the Matron's story, now the *Cena* episode and so on. Different parts appealed to different ages, and the Arbiter is esteemed as a poet, schoolmaster, voluptuary, satirist, near Christian and motion-picture near-villain. Few men have been furnished with so many roles, not the least irony for a devotee of the theater arts. In this capacity, which most truly represents the real Petronius, he has seldom been recognized.

Broadly speaking, it can be said that history has furnished two main conceptions of our author. The first of them regards Petronius as a schoolroom mentor, an authority upon prose and verse usage and, perhaps above all, a source of edifying maxims. The fact, however odd it may appear to us today, is no small tribute to the man's genius. This conception had a long life, prevailing as it did during the later empire and in the so-called Dark Ages and extending into the Middle Ages proper. It ceased to exist when supplanted by the second conception, which came gradually into being with the rediscovery and reassessment of pagan literature which we know as the Renaissance. This latter, which we may call the modern conception, has had a continuous existence, in various vogues and attitudes, until our own day, taking account of Petronius the literary artist, the dilettante, the satirist, the libertine, the storyteller, the courtier, and the man, establishing a tradition which has become firmly fixed in the imagination.

Perhaps neither conception, or even both together, do full justice to the *Satyricon,* as they take no account of Petronius the *Satyricos* as I have attempted to show him in my second chapter. Indeed, there is some reason to believe, as I shall mention below, that our author has been best understood by a venerable cleric of the twelfth century!

We do not know what reputation Petronius enjoyed in his own first century, outside the select circle of his own acquaintance. The second and third centuries most likely paid him scant attention, for they reveal some distaste for their immediate predecessors. Suetonius, writing in the early second century, is another Varro or Elder Pliny, an encyclopedic mind with an obsession for factual details, and his biographies of the Caesars show much disgust for these representatives of an age of cultivated debauchery. Fronto (ca. 100–ca. 166) is rhetoric personified and a determined archaizer, seeking his models far back among the earliest of Rome's authors, Plautus, Ennius, and Cato, and making a point of loathing Seneca, so representative of the first century.

Apuleius, born ca. 123 must, we feel, have known and admired Petronius, but the two are very different, for the African stands for everything which the Arbiter abhorred, the cult of rhetorical device, of archaism, of mysticism, religious fervor and magic.

I *Petronius the Poet*

We know of course from the *Satyricon* itself that Petronius wrote verse, which he interspersed among the prose passages of his work in obedience to the Menippean convention. The bulk of it is in dactylic hexameters, more than four hundred lines in the fragments we possess, including the two hundred and ninety-five of the *Bellum Civile*. There are also twenty-six elegiac couplets, mostly in groups of two and three, four brief bursts in hendecasyllabics, a continuous passage of sixty-five iambic senarii (the *Troiae Halosis*) and a few lines in other meters. It is enough to show that our author was sufficiently accomplished in this normal pastime of a Roman gentleman of leisure. His versification is skillful and facile, lacking the creative genius of his prose writing.

The *Bellum Civile*, owing to its length and to the comparison it affords with Lucan's contemporary epic on the same subject, early attracted attention for its own sake. The qualities and defects of Petronius' contribution to the theme of the struggle for power between Caesar and Pompey have been amply discussed, as also the problem of how far Petronius' verses are to be considered a parody of Lucan's.[2]

Already in the ninth century Petronius' *Bellum* was read and made use of in the monastery of Auxerre in Burgundy where the oldest surviving manuscript of our author's work, the Codex Altissiodurensis, now called the Bernensis, was written towards the close of that century. About the year 876, Heiric, a monk of Auxerre, dedicated a poem on the life of St. Germain to the Emperor Charles the Bald, into which he introduced several quotations and reminiscences of the *Bellum.*

Vincent of Beauvais the encyclopedist,[3] who died about 1264, has several quotations from the *Bellum* in various parts of his *Speculum Historiale*, which he erroneously attributes to a Petronius, Archbishop of Bologna in the fifth century, while William the Breton, also, like Vincent, of the thirteenth century, hints at verse 174 of the *Bellum—indice Fortuna cadat alea*—in the second book of his *Philippid.*

Jean de Montreuil (1354–1418) knows the *Satyricon,* but attributes to Afranius, the writer of domestic comedies in the second century B.C., lines taken from the *Bellum* of Petronius, while Antonino De' Forciglioni (1389–1459), Archbishop of Florence, echoes in his *Opus Historiale* the citations of Vincent of Beauvais, with the same false attribution to Petronius of Bologna. He describes them as *moralia,* edifying maxims for the schoolroom, thus showing the use to which the Arbiter's work was put in his time.

The popularity of the *Bellum* during the fifteenth century is attested by the fact that we possess three manuscripts of this date which contain this part of the *Satyricon* alone. Furthermore, one of the earliest printed editions of Petronius, indeed the first to be published in Germany, contained the *Bellum* only. It is that of Hermann Busch, who ascribes the poem to Petronius Arbiter, Poeta Satyricus. It appeared at Leipzig in 1500 and was reprinted in 1508. A third edition was published at Vienna in 1517 by I. Singrenius and reprinted in 1523.

Janus Dousa (Jan van der Does, 1545–1604), the Dutch historian and poet who was governor of Leyden during its heroic defense against siege in 1574, published in 1583 his famous *Praecidanea,* the first detailed scholarly commentary on Petronius and his work, the forerunner and inspiration of the hundreds which were to follow. He discusses the *Bellum Civile* which he regards as an illustrative criticism of Lucan. He prefers Petronius' poem to the Spaniard's.

The vogue continued. In 1658 a handsome edition containing

both poems was produced at Amsterdam by Cornelius Schrevelius, while in 1675 a direct imitation of Petronius' *Bellum* took the form of a *Guerre Espagnole* by Sarrasin, printed in Paris.

The first translation into French of any part of the *Satyricon* was a prose version of the *Bellum* by Michel de Marolles, combined with a translation of Lucan, which appeared in 1654. About the same time an Italian verse translation had been written by one Giovanni Argoli, apparently unpublished. Various other renderings are recorded as belonging to the seventeenth century, while in the eighteenth, Francesco Algarotti caused quite a stir with his version of 1740 which was debated and criticized by a group of scholar friends who seem not to have shared the enthusiasm roused in the sixteenth and seventeenth centuries for the poets of Nero's court. But the Italians, until modern times, have been far less lavish in their praise of Petronius than the French, preserving a more strictly moral attitude towards him than that accorded by their neighbors, who have always shown indulgence regarding the Arbiter whose wit is so like their own. Algarotti's critics, taking note of a verse translation of the *Bellum* by a president of the French Academy, Jean Bouhier, published in 1737, admitted that Petronius went better into French than into Italian.

These details, together with later data on the fortunes of the *Bellum Civile*, are fully presented by Anthony Rini in his book *Petronius in Italy*,[4] to which the reader is referred. I have mentioned enough to show that this portion of the *Satyricon* has enjoyed a success of itself and by itself through the centuries.

We do not know what other writings in prose or verse were produced by the Arbiter besides the *Satyricon*, but we learn from the grammarian Terentianus Maurus who, towards the end of the third century A.D., wrote a treatise on meter, that Petronius made frequent use of the anacreontic type of verse, an iambic dimeter catalectic named after the Greek lyric poet of the sixth century B.C. Terentianus quotes two couplets, referring to Egyptian boys and girls participating in religious festivals, which he tells us are still sung in his own day.[5] The remark is significant as showing that our author enjoyed a vogue as lyric poet two centuries and more after his death, a fact confirmed by two other grammarians, Marius Victorinus and Diomedes, writing in the fourth century, who also quote examples of Petronius' anacreontics.[6]

The fifth-century Gallo-Roman panegyrist Sidonius Apollinaris[7] refers to the Arbiter as a votary of Priapus, which would imply that he gained fame as a writer of *Priapea,* poems in honor of the fertility god. Such poems were a fashionable pastime. Catullus, Tibullus, Horace, Virgil, Ovid, and Martial tried their hand at them, and we possess some eighty or so collected in the first century A.D. In view of our author's preoccupation with things Priapic in the *Satyricon,* it is not surprising that critics of the later empire should acknowledge him in this capacity.

A number of manuscripts have preserved verses, mainly elegiac couplets, hexameters, and hendecasyllabics which, because of style or content, have been attributed by scholars through the ages to Petronius. Some of these are indeed probably isolated fragments of the *Satyricon* itself, belonging either to known or unknown episodes of the work. They are cited in the appendices of the principal editions of our author.

Such of his verse as has come down to us would hardly establish for Petronius today a claim to independent fame thereby. But the fact that the commentators of the empire pay tribute to him as a poet of anacreontic and priapeian (probably chiefly hendecasyllabic) verse shows that he was esteemed by them as an authority on such matters.

II *Petronius the Authority on Language*

Not only in the realm of versification and metrics is Petronius an authority for scholars in late imperial times. He is cited by the fourth-century grammarian Servius, the famous commentator on Virgil, on more than one occasion as an authority on correct forms and spellings of words. From this it is clear that our author was considered a master of Latin prose style at this time, a model to be studied, a sure guide in matters of usage. The fifth, sixth and seventh centuries continue to regard him as such. Sidonius mentioned him as one of the glories of Latin verbal expression, linking his name with those of Cicero, Livy, and Virgil, while the enormously influential Priscian, the important theologian Fulgentius, and the great philosopher Boethius, himself a practitioner of the Menippean genre, all quote Petronius as an authority on usage. In the seventh century, the encyclopedist Isidore of Seville also makes use of the Arbiter.

All these men exerted tremendous influence on succeeding generations and so carried Petronius' fame with them right into and throughout the Middle Ages.

III *The Moralist*

Ecclesiastical authority in the Middle Ages, in whose sole keeping lay the sources of all knowledge of the ancient world and the means of its diffusion, was genuinely concerned to preserve what it considered to be the good element in the writings of the pagan authors, especially when the latter were acknowledged masters of that Latin speech which was the Church's official language, through which its teachings were propagated.

We have seen that during the late empire and in the Dark Ages Petronius was one of these acknowledged masters, and we may be sure that from the fourth or fifth century dates the epitomized version which for those days conferred the cachet of distinction upon a classical author and from which our present fragments descend.

And yet this epitome contained all too much that the all-powerful Church of later centuries could not condone. However, keen observer of human nature and shrewd judge of its foibles as he was, Petronius had written into his lascivious novel many a remark which, taken from its context, would serve admirably as moral instruction for the young minds in the Church's care to whom access to the *Satyricon* itself must be denied.

Thus, our author finds himself in the company of his admired Publilius Syrus, the master of that mime tradition so dear to himself, as a source of educational pabulum for the medieval schoolboy.[8] It is a supreme irony that both are on the same bookshelf with old Cato, the prototype of the puritanical spirit in defiance of which the *Satyricon* was penned.

The innocuous nature of the moral maxims taken from the Arbiter is shown by the fact that they were attributed, as we have mentioned above, to Petronius of Bologna, who, besides being an archbishop, was also a saint! The error is due to Vincent of Beauvais and was merely repeated by Forciglioni two centuries later.

The *moralia* cited by Vincent and reproduced by Forciglioni include such sentiments as "Of what use are the laws when money alone is king?" (*Satyricon,* 14.2); "It is dangerous to be a party to another's secrets" (20.3); "Beauty and wisdom do not go together" (94.1); "Poverty, it so happens, is the sister of Virtue" (84.4); "The votes of the populace incline towards profit and the chink of coin; the people are venal, the courts of justice especially are venal and authority itself will surrender to the corruption of gold" (119, verses 40–41, 44); "He who has money may sail with a safe passage and may direct his fate according to his will" (137.9).

These cynical pronouncements of our author in his satirical vein enjoyed a continuous vogue through the centuries, and one or the other of them, especially the first and the last, are often recalled by editors in the preface to their editions and commentaries published in those times when Petronius was chiefly regarded as a satirist.

The Middle Ages too had a strong satiric bent, particularly evident on the outer fringe of the ecclesiastical world. The dispossessed clerics, who pen their vitriolic verses denouncing the avarice and injustice of the hierarchy, echo Petronius' sentiments in astonishingly similar language. However, we may be sure that the intention of Vincent and other compilers of Petronian *dicta* in the Middle Ages was not to fan discontent against the Church but to instruct the youth in its care, while at the same time preserving what was fit to preserve of a notable pagan author.

IV *"All the World's a Stage"*

Vincent's citations range across the whole extent of the *Satyricon* as we ourselves know it today, except that they do not include anything from the *Cena* episode. Perhaps this part of the work was not available in the manuscripts (supposing that he had more than one) to which Vincent had access. Nevertheless, the *Cena*, at least in part, was known in the thirteenth century, for the anthology of various Latin authors known as the *Florilegium Parisinum* (cod. Paris. lat. 17903),[9] which contains some half dozen or so *dicta* from the *Cena* among its Petroniana, was copied early in that century. Indeed, the Middle Ages in all probability possessed at least as much of Petronius as we, although in isolated manuscripts known only to this or that small group of scholars at some cathedral court or in some monastic community which happened to possess one.

Special mention must be made of the twelfth-century Englishman John of Salisbury, author of the famous critical study of court life and the duties of kingship and administration known as the *Policraticus.*[10] In his youth John had studied in France, notably at Chartres and at Paris and with great assiduity and profit, under the greatest scholars of his day, including Abelard and Bernard of Clairvaux. The latter recommended him to the service of Theobald, Archbishop of Canterbury, whose secretary he became in 1147. On the death of Theobald in 1162, John continued as secretary to his successor, Thomas Becket, whom he loyally served to his own cost in the conflict between Becket and King Henry II over the rival claims of ecclesiastical and regal privilege. He was present in Canterbury Cathedral when the archbishop was murdered there by Henry's knights on December 29, 1170. Six years later he became Bishop of Chartres, where he died in 1180.

John was one of the most learned scholars of Latin literature of his own or indeed any age. His satirical temperament delighted particularly in Horace, Juvenal, and Petronius to whom he twice refers as "our Arbiter" and to whose work there are more than twenty allusions in his writings.[11] More than once does he mention Trimalchio and his banquet, and in particular he recalls the incident of the invention of unbreakable glass (*Satyricon,* 51; *Policraticus,* 4.5.521 b). He also reproduces the story of the Matron of Ephesus (*Satyricon,* 111–112; *Policraticus,* 8.11.753b). But these are not the most significant of his reminiscences of the *Satyricon.*

It is no exaggeration to say that John of Salisbury shows a more complete understanding of Petronius than that attained by any other creative writer, be he satirist or romancer, or any critic or commentator before or since his time. The reason for this unique insight lies in the fact that in John's own twelfth century, and particularly in the milieu in which he found himself, the theatrical tradition which Petronius the *Satyricos* represents was still very much alive.

From the Renaissance onwards, both admiration and criticism of the Arbiter were largely conditioned by the conception of him as the gay, dissolute courtier of Nero, and the interpretation of the *Satyricon* has right up to modern times been too narrowly affected by this conception. For this error the portrait given by Tacitus in Book 16 of the *Annals* is responsible.

John of Salisbury was thoroughly acquainted with the writings of many of the great Latin authors, Cicero, Sallust, Virgil, Horace, Quintilian, Ovid, Seneca, Lucan, Martial, Juvenal, Pliny the

Elder, Suetonius, to name but a few. But of Tacitus he knew nothing, except the bare name, for no manuscript of the historian appears to have been known in the twelfth century, at least in centers of active scholarship.

John is concerned to show in his *Policraticus* that the pursuit of wisdom and virtue is essential to the regal function and to proper government. To this end he devotes five of his eight books on the subject (I–III, VII and VIII) to a detailed condemnation of those inept and vicious preoccupations which detract from man's natural dignity and undermine his capacity to fulfill God's purpose for him in this life by obscuring his self-knowledge, impairing his powers of discipline, and deluding his judgment with the false sense of security engendered by indulgence in sensual pleasures.

Now it is quite possible that Canterbury's learned secretary had no notion that the author of the *Satyricon* was a member of Nero's court. He may indeed have supposed that Petronius belonged to a later century than the first. What he does clearly see, as later generations did not, is the world of theatrical make-believe which the Roman so vividly presents. In all probability John does not realize, as we do, that the Arbiter is more a sympathetic observer and participant than a censorious critic. His medieval viewpoint would incline him to regard Petronius as a satirical moralist, a milder Juvenal. In this, but in this alone, we have the advantage over the twelfth century. John's contemporaries lived in a world far closer to that of Petronius than our own, not merely in time (hardly relevant) but most significantly in thought, since pagan traditions and habits were still patently alive and influential on all levels of society. About Petronius the satirist John may have been in error; about Petronius the *satyricos* he was more aware than we.

The greatest obstacle to self-knowledge is pride, and John is particularly concerned in his third book to denounce that abiding evil of court life, the flatterer, the enemy of all virtue as he calls him. Against his poisonous blandishments John cites the testimony of the ancient writers and the Scriptures, and at the end of Chapter 7 he quotes in full the Arbiter's famous verses on the treacherous nature of the friendship which attends upon good fortune and is assumed and discarded like the comedian's mask (*Satyricon*, 80).

Society resembles a play which a troupe performs upon a stage.

The parts are assumed only for so long as they are needed. When fortune deserts the patron, the flatterer puts off the mask of friendship and reveals his true face.

The flatterer deceives his patron and is himself inured by habitual practice into self-deception. The patron becomes so enamored of adulation that he cannot shake off the false image of himself. Comedy, says John, portrays the life of man on earth and that life itself becomes a play where each man forgets his real identity and lives another's part. Petronius speaks truly when he declares that almost the whole world can be seen to be indulging in a mime (*fere totus mundus ex Arbitri nostri sententia mimum videtur implere*) with the result that they cannot return to their true selves when necessary, even as children who, having perfected themselves in the imitation of stammerers, find that they can no longer speak properly when they want to (*Policraticus,* 3.8).

The ambitious clerk in the service of king, prelate, or noble is all too prone to become a flatterer and parasite and this John wishes to make clear. But he does not speak of the illusions of the theater merely in a figurative sense. Actual theatrical performances were very much a part of the private life of king and noble in the twelfth century. In addition to the professional parasite who earned his keep by his wits as jester and clown, the descendant of the classical *scurra,* troupes of players of mime and *fabula* were maintained as part of the permanent establishment of the households of the great, and John speaks of them at length in his first book. Together with conjurers, magicians, and astrologers, they are a great menace to their masters, inducing in them a love of fantasy, luxury, lasciviousness, and pagan superstition fatal to good government and to spiritual progress alike.

For excessive indulgence in the theater arts leads to certain damnation of the soul, maintains John, the voice of ecclesiastical authority. The majority, Petronius' *fere totus mundus,* who surrender to the enticement of self-deception, will not be counted among the seven thousand whom the Lord has kept for himself, all the knees which have not bowed unto Baal (*Policraticus,* 3.8; I Kings, 19.18). These elect, whose salvation is assured, will despise the theater which is the world and the plays staged therein by fickle Fortune (*Policraticus,* 3.10).

Thus then does this leading spirit of the twelfth century, one of the privileged few to whom classical learning is available in those times, understand the essentially escapist nature of the world of the *Satyricon*. Ironically, John did not know that it was also Petronius' world, since he did not know that the Arbiter was himself a courtier and the intimate companion of an emperor who lived almost perpetually among the unreal fantasies of his feverish imagination. He often mentions Nero, whose vices are familiar to him from the pages of Suetonius, but is unable to link him with our author. Nevertheless, the satyric significance of Petronius' work comes clearly through to one whose own observation of life around him makes him lament that "all the world's a stage. . . ." [12]

Hypocrisy is the constant theme of the *Satyricon*, and literally of course the word means "acting a part." All the characters of Petronius are concerned most of the time in some form of deception, either of others or of themselves. Trimalchio puts on a constant show to dazzle his guests and is perhaps deceived as to their admiration of him. Encolpius assumes the part of a *scholasticus* to earn a meal and plays the part badly. Giton deceives now one, now the other of his lovers. Eumolpus is incapable of straightforward conduct and a master of self-deception to boot. All our heroes join in a grandiose deception of the Crotonians who themselves beguile and flatter, a community of legacy hunters. The famous remark, seized upon by John and echoed by Shakespeare, is prompted by the twofold treachery of Ascyltos and Giton. Petronius the pagan accepts this behavior as essential in human nature, necessitated by the pursuit of happiness, man's legitimate goal. John the Christian condemns it as contrary to the divine purpose.

V *The Matron of Ephesus*

In Chapter 11 of his eighth book of the *Policraticus* John discourses at length upon the trials and dangers of marriage. For him woman is something of a necessary evil, and he cites with evident satisfaction the strictures of the philosophers and Church Fathers at her expense. To illustrate the fickleness of the sex no example could be more fruitful than the story of the Matron of Ephesus which he relates in full, as it is given by Petronius in Chapters 111 and 112 of the *Satyricon*.

Not least of the paradoxes which confront us when we consider the influence of Petronius through the centuries is that his greatest claim to fame on this score has been the transmission of a Milesian tale. The magnificently creative artist whose brilliant evocative powers are allied to a style whose facility and polish are unexcelled in Latin literature has exerted his influence chiefly through something which is not really his own. Indeed he was not even first with it upon the Roman scene, for the fabulist Phaedrus,[13] who died some fifteen years before our author, has the tale in his repertoire. Probably, like the story of unbreakable glass and the Civil War and the capture of Troy themes, it enjoyed a vogue in the first century. But in various forms the story belongs to a most ancient Indo-European tradition which itself may have borrowed the details from the Far East. Thus the account of a fair woman's infidelity to her dead husband spread gradually westwards from some cradle of civilization, if indeed it did not spring up spontaneously in different regions.[14]

However odd it may seem, this short anecdote, less than one-fortieth of the *Satyricon* as it has survived, has enjoyed a fame far greater in terms of duration than the *Cena* episode, which the name of Petronius now chiefly calls to mind. This is partly due to the fact that the *Cena* in its complete form was not rediscovered until the seventeenth century, but it was nevertheless to some extent known in the Middle Ages when certainly it was eclipsed in popularity by the Matron.

The reason is not far to seek. The *Cena* is highly topical, a slice of freedman parvenu life in Campania in the first century, and, whether so recognized or not in the absence of information regarding its author, its appeal was not for every age. But every age does love a tale which satirizes womankind and combines humor with a little moral instruction, to be taken as required. The Middle Ages was the epoch par excellence for merry tales, fabliaux, and facetiae, and the Matron's story is a favorite among them.

However, it must not be thought that Petronius has the sole, or even the principal credit for its diffusion. The first appearance of the Matron in Italian, for example, is in the anonymous collection known as *Il Novellino*,[15] a hundred tales or *novelle* of the late thirteenth century, of which it is the fifty-ninth. The details of this version are quite different from those given by our author and may well have come from some earlier collection of Aesopian fables or from a version of Phaedrus or from the numerous compilations in Latin, French, and Italian called the *Book of the*

Seven Sages (*Liber Septem Sapientium*).[16] A fourteenth-century Italian writer of *novelle,* Sercambi, also has a version of the Matron.

The evidence is that numerous medieval renderings of the story owed nothing at all to Petronius. It is significant that Boccaccio, who certainly knew our author, if only through Fulgentius the mythographer, nowhere reveals in his tales of love or elsewhere any clearly discernible influence of him. It would appear that only John of Salisbury possessed sufficient of the text of Petronius to stimulate interest and quotation. There did exist in the twelfth century a manuscript of Petronius containing the Matron alone, the Codex Parisinus Mazarinaeus 1261, and indeed this may be the source from which John took his account of the story, since the codex also contains parts of Boethius and of Seneca to whom he refers from time to time. But doubtless this source was unknown to the compilers of *novelle,* with whom therefore we are not concerned, since they do not use Petronius. It may be mentioned in passing, for example, that the version of the Matron's story which is number 33 of the famous *Fables* of Marie de France,[17] written about 1190, owes nothing to Petronius, but was derived, like many others of the collection, from an English prose translation of the fourth-century fabulist Romulus whose material in turn was derived from Phaedrus' *Aesop.*

The invention of printing of course made our author, like the other great classical writers, available to the general literate public, although the *editio princeps,* which saw the light of day at Milan in 1482, aroused little interest in spite of the fact that its editor was the accomplished scholar Puteolanus or Francesco dal Pozzo, professor of rhetoric at Bologna, where in 1471 he had published the first edition of Ovid. Stimulus to Petronian studies in the fifteenth century had arisen from the discovery by Poggio of two manuscripts of our author in 1420 and 1423. A second edition of the fragments appeared at Venice in 1499, largely, if not entirely, based upon the first.

A number of Italian scholars in the fifteenth century showed keen admiration for Petronius, including the notable teacher Filippo Beroaldo (1453–1505), a pupil of Puteolanus. But in the following century in Italy interest in him declined, probably because the fragmentary nature of his work and its immoral content caused him to be overshadowed by the greater figures of the classical world that the Renaissance was eagerly rediscovering. No new edition was forthcoming in Italy during the sixteenth century, while France produced her first, by Regnault-Chaudière, in 1520 at Paris, while that of Jean de Tournes and the two by Pierre Pithou followed in 1575, 1577, and 1578 respectively. They had been preceded in 1565 by the edition of Sambucus, printed at Antwerp. In Germany the *Bellum Civile* had already been printed at Leipzig in 1500.

Thus gradually the foundations were laid for a critical appreciation of our author, who begins to emerge as a personality. Pithou in his first edition of 1577 conjectures that the author of the *Satyricon* is the Petronius of whom Tacitus speaks in the *Annals*. The ball begins to roll and gathers accretions from the pen of famous scholar-critics like Janus Dousa, Joseph Scaliger, and Justus Lipsius.

The result is that Petronius comes into his own as the wittiest source for the Matron's tale. Its dramatic possibilities become apparent, so that we have the Englishman George Chapman, poet, classical scholar, and playwright (1557–1634), who had collaborated with Ben Jonson and Marston to produce *Eastward Hoe,* putting on in 1605 *The Widow's Tears, a Comedy.*[18] This early play is typical of the many which were to follow. With five acts and a cast of seventeen, it contains much that owes nothing whatever to Petronius. The theme is familiar to Elizabethan drama, the testing of a wife's fidelity to her husband by a plot against her chastity. The husband's brother plays upon his jealousy with coarse insinuation:

THARSALIO: Only your blockheadly tradesman, your honest-meaning citizen, your knot-headed country-gentleman; your unapprehending stinkard, is blest with the sole prerogative of his wife's chamber; for which he is yet beholden, not to his stars, but to his ignorance: for if he be wise, brother, I must tell you, the case alters. How do you relish these things, brother?

LYSANDER: Passing ill.

THARSALIO: So do sick men solid meats. Heark ye, brother, are you not jealous?

LYSANDER: No: do you know cause to make me?

THARSALIO: Hold you there; did your wife never spice your broth with a dram of sublimate? Hath she not yielded up the fort of her honor to a staring soldado? and (taking courage from her guilt) plaid open bankrupt of all shame, and run the country with him? Then bless your stars, bow your knees to Juno. (Act I, Sc. 7)

But there are genuine echoes of Petronius' language, as in the remark of Lycus to Lysander: "The world hath written your wife in highest lines of honor'd fame; her virtues so admir'd in this isle [Cyprus], as the report thereof sounds in foreign ears; and strangers oft arriving here [as some rare sight] desire to view her presence, thereby to compare the picture with the original." (II.2).

Lysander allows himself to become party to the plot, whereby he is alleged to have been murdered. His wife and her serving maid betake themselves to his supposed tomb to keep watch until death shall claim them also. Here too (Act IV, Sc. 2) the language, as well as the situation, recalls our author: "Five days thus hast she wasted; and not once season'd her palate with the taste of meat, her powers of life are spent; and what remains of her famish'd spirit, serves not to breathe, but sigh."

Lysander has disguised himself as a soldier, to attempt his wife's constancy and virtue:

> Lady, I am centinel,
> Set in this hallowed place, to watch and guard
> On forfeit of my life, these monuments
> From rape, and spoil of sacrilegious hands;
> And save the bodies, that without you see,
> Of crucified offenders; that no friends
> May bear them hence to honour'd burial.

He succeeds in his purpose, as did Petronius' soldier, and the wife is only too anxious to save him from punishment for the neglect of his duties by substituting the corpse in the tomb for one which has been stolen (by Tharsalio) from the cross. At this point the plot ceases to follow Petronius, for the conspirators are caught and haled off to court.

In 1614 appeared *L'Ephésienne,* probably written by Pierre Mainfray of Rouen,[19] which acknowledges Petronius as its source, although, as with Chapman's play, there is much added detail of plot and characterization. It is an excellent piece of work, with subtle dramatic and psychological development, the verse facile and eloquent. Chapman's widow engages in an unseemly struggle with her disguised husband to get at the corpse. Mainfray's Astasie is more dignified, but gives a helping hand all the same:

> Prenez par là Frontin, et nous deux par ici,
> Nous le souleverons,

and she gives the soldier good advice as to how to arrange the body on the gibbet:

> Courbez luy bien la teste afin que chacun pense
> Que c'est le mesme corps que l'on y avoit mis.

On May 12, 1682, the king's Italian players performed *La Matrone d'Ephèse,* a three-act comedy in prose, which is indebted to Petronius in only one scene. The author was Noland de Fatouville. Other dramatic versions of the story are those of la Motte 1702, Fuselier 1714, Legay 1788, Watelet and Isaac Bickerstaff about the same date, and Radet 1792. In more recent times, Mulè's verse drama *La Sposa di Efeso,* produced in 1923, was highly successful, and of course the story has had many one-act representations on amateur and private stages right up to our own day. A public performance which received warm praise in spite of wartime conditions was that put on at the Théâtre du Parc in Brussels by Georges Sion in 1943, during the German occupation.

But it was in seventeenth-century France that the Matron enjoyed her greatest vogue and the freethinking libertines of the court circle loved to read, translate, and imitate Petronius' account of her. Saint-Evremond's delightful rendering was included in La Fontaine's *Nouvelles en vers* (1665) and in the *Jugement sur Sénèque, Plutarque et Pétrone* (1670). For Saint-Evremond, Petronius is "le seul de l'antiquité qui ait su parler de galanterie," and he praises the Arbiter's death as the noblest in antiquity. That other *enfant terrible* of the age, Bussy-Rabutin, who found himself in jail for his scandalous *Histoire amoureuse des Gaules,* was a very reincarnation of our author, and he too translated the Matron in 1677, to the great admiration of his friends.

Surely the Matron found her apotheosis in La Fontaine's exquisite *La Matrone d'Ephèse,* now number 6 of the fifth part of his

Contes, published in 1682. Here, in the grace of language and delicacy of humor our author has met his match:

> Dans Ephèse il fut autrefois
> Une dame en sagesse et vertus sans égale
> Et, selon la commune voix
> Ayant sceu rafiner sur l'amour conjugale.
> Il n'étoit bruit que d'elle et de sa chasteté;
> On l'alloit voir par rareté;
> C'étoit l'honneur du sexe: heureuse sa patrie!
> Chaque mère à sa bru l'alleguoit pour patron;
> Chaque époux la prônoit à sa femme chérie:
> D'elle descendent ceux de la Prudoterie,
> Antique et célèbre maison.

Instead of the summary justice which earlier morality had thought necessary, although not on Petronius' authority, La Fontaine echoes the sentiments of his day and is full of indulgence for the offender:

> Car de mettre au patibulaire
> Le corps d'un mary tant aimé,
> Ce n'étoit pas peut-être une si grande affaire:
> Cela luy sauvoit l'autre; et, tout considéré,
> Mieux vaut goujat debout qu'empereur enterré.

Later translations and imitations of the Matron are less faithful to the Arbiter. The Italian Manfredi (1674–1739), in his prose adaptation, obviously enjoys embellishing the story with much detail of his own, while his fellow countryman Cosimo Scotti, in the early nineteenth century, prolongs his account in a revival of *novelle* à la Boccaccio.

Enough has been said to indicate that Petronius has been kept very much alive in the imagination of the centuries through the Milesian Tale which he thought fit to reproduce as an example of Eumolpus' talents. In conclusion it must be said that critical investigation has sometimes exaggerated in seeking to ascribe to the Ephesian lady, whether under the aegis of the Arbiter or no, an influence which examination must refute. Thus, the sixth chapter of Alphonse Daudet's *L'Immortel*, which has a scene of a lovers' meeting in a family vault, has been thought to echo the situation of the Milesian. But there is no hint whatsoever in the details of the action or the language to recall a resemblance. Similarly, Paul Alexis' story *Après la Bataille,* in the collection of reminiscences of the Franco-Prussian War entitled *Les Soirées de Médan,*[20] has been said to owe a debt to the Matron's story. A young woman, transporting in a wagon the body of her husband, killed in battle, gives a lift to a wounded soldier. She dresses his wound, and they converse. They are attracted to each other, and, encompassed by nightfall, they yield to a sudden desire, seeking release from pain and grief. In this brief wartime episode there is absolutely nothing of Petronius or Phaedrus.

VI *John Barclay's* Euphormio

On the British side of the Channel Petronius is almost exclusively thought of as a satirist. John of Salisbury derived his classical training and his philosophical ideas mainly from the Continent. The tradition of the English universities tended to assimilate the Arbiter to Horace, Juvenal, Persius, and Martial, and he shares the general approval accorded to these castigators of moral decadence. Such contrasting geniuses as Jeremy Taylor and Ben Jonson[21] share a warm admiration for Petronius. Swift, of course, must have found much that was congenial in the Roman. Pope noted that "Fancy and art in gay Petronius please, The scholar's learning, with the courtier's ease" (*Essay on Criticism,* 667–68), than which no neater summary of our author's talents exists. For Dryden he was "the most elegant and one of the most judicious authors of the Latin tongue" (*Essay of Heroic Plays*), the sound judgment of the expert on the Roman satirists, the renowned translator of the classics.

Towards the end of the eighteenth century perhaps Petronius was less in favor, for Dr. Johnson seems to have approved of Joseph Warton's sneers at "this dissolute and effeminate writer," à propos of Pope's eulogy in his edition of the latter's works (1797). At any rate, poor William Cowper, the tender poet of nature who had the misfortune to turn his hand to satire, was certainly wrongheaded about the Arbiter.

> Petronius! all the muses weep for thee;
> But ev'ry tear shall scald thy memory:
> Thou polish'd and high finish'd foe to truth,

Grey-beard corruptor of our list'ning youth,
To purge and skim away the filth of vice,
That, so refin'd, it might the more entice,
Then pour it on the morals of thy son,
To taint his heart, was worthy of thine own!

Thus he wrote in *The Progress of Error* (1782). But Petronius was not Lord Chesterfield!

Far nearer to the spirit of the *Satyricon* were those improvident and harassed Grub-Street hack journalists and broadsheet poets who flourished, if that be the word, at the beginning of the eighteenth century.[22] They closely resemble in their calling and in their enthusiasm for the classics, with which they never fail to lace their political satire, those would-be court poets, more often akin to wandering scholars, at the tail end of the Elizabethan age, men like Everard Guilpin, Thomas Bastard, John Weever, and Samuel Rowlands, who poured out "centuries" of epigrams in the manner of Martial. Typical of the journalists round about 1700 was Tom Brown of Shifnal, who left his native Shropshire to tempt Fortune in London. Among his other activities, he was an ardent translator of the classics and collaborated in a translation of Petronius, published in 1708, four years after his death.

But we must return to the end of Elizabeth's reign (1603), there to find the curious figure of John Barclay, the author of the closest imitation of Petronius which history affords, the *Satyricon Euphormionis,* the first part of which appeared in London in 1603 with a dedication to the new monarch, James I (1603–1625).[23]

John Barclay was born in 1582 at Pont-à-Mousson in Lorraine where his father William Barclay occupied the chair of law at the university. The family was a notable one, belonging to Aberdeenshire in Scotland. John also studied law and traveled much, ambitious to make his name and to secure patronage. Having so to speak welcomed the new sovereign, Scotland's own James VI, to England as the first of the name, he left London in 1604 and stayed awhile at Angers where he composed the second part of the *Euphormio*, dedicated to Robert Cecil, son of William Lord Burghley, Elizabeth's great minister. In 1605 John was in Paris, where he married. In 1606 he arrived back in London for a stay of ten years, consolidating his position at court as a Gentleman of the Royal Chamber. 1616 saw him in Rome where he composed his popular romance, the *Argenis*, finished just before his death in 1621.

The *Euphormio* contains an autobiographical element, based partly on the misfortunes of John's father William, who had been forced into exile as a loyal supporter of Mary Stuart. But John declares himself to be Euphormio, who, himself an exile from mythical Lusinia, is forced to sell himself into slavery to a nouveau-riche, Callio (an echo of Trimalchio), who forthwith conveys him to his splendid residence. There he is at first ill-treated but finds a friend in a fellow slave, Percas. In the relationship between these two there is much to recall the partnership of Encolpius and Ascyltos. Percas advises him to feign madness, which he does, and Callio treats him with a drug compounded of various magical ingredients to which a pearl and an emerald are added. Euphormio pretends that the mixture has done the trick and returns to his senses. Callio, highly pleased, despatches Euphormio and Percas to an invalid friend Fibullius, to attempt his cure, and thus begin the wanderings of the hero and his companion, which take them to various localities bearing classical names, like Basilea and Ilium, but which, according to commentators, may be identified with places in France, the Low Countries, and Italy.

The adventures which befall them are many and fantastic, in the manner of Greek romance, but with much satire and burlesque and in the convention of Menippus, for there are many incursions into verse, especially in the earlier part of the narrative. Barclay is thoroughly indebted to Petronius, and there are many direct imitations of the Arbiter, both in incident and language. Shortly after setting out on their journey to Fibullius, there is an encounter with a sorceress and her attendants which is full of reminiscences of the Priapic revels of Quartilla and of the dire remedies of the old crone Oenothea.

Next on the scene, on the way to Basilea, whose inhabitants are referred to in language recalling Petronius' description of the Crotonians, we meet Barclay's Eumolpus, one Acignius. The name is an anagram of Ignatius, by whom is meant Ignatius Loyola, the founder of the Society of Jesus. He and his followers are satirized in the Acignians, of whom Euphormio seeks instruction in an episode he later recalls, in the second part of the work, when safely arrived in Scolymorhodia (Thistle-Rose land, i.e. Great Britain). The Acignians were established in Delphia (Pont-à-Mousson) and would have made him one of theirs, had not Theophrastus (Cardinal du Perron) intervened, so that our hero fled to Marcia (Venice), where the Jesuits were not admitted.

The *Satyricon* of Barclay is tediously prolonged and is full of political and religious parody and satire. The author is keen to display his virtuosity and his command of Latin, to rival and outdo his Roman model in versatility and inventiveness. Always does he pay him the sincerest flattery by the closest possible imitation. What is more important for us is the fact that Barclay undoubtedly knew, not only the pre- and post-*Cena* episodes, but also the *Cena* itself, from which he frequently borrows both incident and phraseology. The Traù manuscript, containing Trimalchio's feast entire and about which I shall speak in the next section, was not discovered until fifty years after Barclay wrote his *Satyricon.* We can only suppose that he had access to one or more manuscripts as yet unpublished. Pierre Pithou (1539–1596), who prepared two new editions of Petronius in 1577 and 1587, is supposed to have possessed at least six, including the original complete Auxerre manuscript. It is not impossible that Barclay had access to them.

The *Satyricon,* like the *Argenis* and the *Mirror of Minds* (*Icon Animorum*), the other principal works of the wandering Scot, enjoyed immediate popularity and has known a number of editions and translations.

VII *The Rediscovery of the* Cena

A major event in the Petronius story and one which gave a new impetus to Petronian studies, resulting in a spate of commentaries, translations, imitations, and even forgeries of our author, was the discovery in a small township on the Dalmatian coast in the mid-seventeenth century of a manuscript containing the *Cena* episode of the *Satyricon* well-nigh entire. This manuscript, commonly known as the Codex Traguriensis, now officially the Parisinus 7989, is still our only source of the complete *Cena.*[24]

This discovery projected a much fuller image of the Arbiter upon the world's consciousness. His personality is henceforth indissolubly linked with the courtier of Tacitus, himself only recently become known as never before since antiquity. Petronius' wonderfully phrased ironical dicta were after all commonplaces of human experience, the lascivious doings of Quartilla and the wandering students, the splendid hypocrisies of Eumolpus, the shipboard adventures and the Odyssey among the fortune hunters were a delightful parody of Greek romance. But, like the exquisite rendering of the Milesian tale of the Matron, they had a slight flavor of the second-hand. The gorgeously detailed, scintillating burlesque of lower-class provincial life in first-century Italy, which now burst upon a public that had long yearned for its finding, belonged much more to the world of reality and brought men close to its artist creator who had so obviously observed it at first hand.

The facts of the finding of the Traù MS have often been told, following the account given by Giovanni Lucio, a scholar of Traù, in his *Historical Memoirs of Tragurium*, published in 1673. Briefly they are as follows:

A student of jurisprudence, one Marino Statileo, had recently returned to Traù, in about 1650, after taking his doctorate at the University of Padua. Feeling in scholarly mood, he began to work his way through the library of a learned friend Niccolò Cippico, himself a notable Tragurian. He there came across a manuscript containing, among other classical material, Petronius. Whether he himself realized its importance is not clear, but his curiosity was sufficiently roused for him to show the work to Lucio and to another friend, Francesco Dragazzo. The three of them got to grips with the manuscript and compared it with an edition of Petronius they possessed. Between them they realized that here was something new, the whole text of the *Cena.*

In 1654 Lucio left Traù for Italy and began to talk of the discovery. The Venetian ambassador at Rome was excited and ordered a copy of the find which he eventually got published at Padua in 1664. Further copies were printed in Paris and in Amsterdam.

The Padua publication, giving such information as was then known about the discovery, informed the public that the new manuscript was thought to have belonged to Ettore Cippico, a distant forbear of Niccolò, a noted scholar of his day. For all we know, this Ettore may have flourished on the Italian mainland in the fifteenth century at the time the manuscript was compiled, and he may be the person who first acquired it into private possession, whereby it remained in the Cippico family until 1650 when Statileo found it.

Much controversy followed upon the publication of the new findings. Statileo's relative obscurity cast doubt in the minds of not a few, whose jealousy was also aroused by the young man's success. A Frenchman, Adrien Valois, and a German, Christoph Wagenseil, both produced dissertations in 1666, attempting to prove forgery. They were promptly answered by a defense published in the name of Statileo. The original manuscript arrived in Rome in 1668 and was examined by a group of scholars at the house of the Venetian ambassador. They apparently failed to notice the date, November 20, 1423, which the document bears, and assigned it to the fourteenth century, concluding that it must be genuine.

Fortified by this assurance, Statileo's friend Lucio prepared an edition of the Petronian contents of the Traù manuscript which was published together with Statileo's defense at Amsterdam in 1670. The printer dedicated the work to Louis Bourbon, the Prince Condé, who had for some years shown great interest in the controversy. The weight of his illustrious name gave authenticity to the proceedings, and indeed the new edition was justly praised for its value and accuracy. For the time at any rate it silenced critics. But the excitement caused by the Traù discovery led to the hope and expectation of new finds to complete the *Satyricon*.

Demand led to supply, and rumors of fresh Petroniana hidden away in private hands arose and were refuted. Quite a sensation followed the report by a French army officer, François Nodot, to the president of the French Academy that he had come by new fragments of our author, found by another officer at the capture of Belgrade in 1688. In 1692 Nodot published the *Satyricon* with the new additions. Reprints followed the next year, and there was a translation, also by Nodot, which enjoyed even more success, going through several editions in the seventeenth, eighteenth, and nineteenth centuries.[25] But the alleged new fragments were a forgery, obvious as such to scholars really acquainted with Petronius and his style. Yet the affair provoked as much discussion and even more acrimony than the genuine find at Traù.

By the end of the seventeenth century the Arbiter, now clearly identified with Nero's courtier, was a well-known figure in the literary world, greatly appreciated in France, rather unpopular in Italy which preserved a straitlaced attitude towards his lascivious content. Queen Christina of Sweden (1626–1689) is said to have preferred our author to all others.[26]

VIII *The Eighteenth Century*

Mention of Queen Christina serves to remind us that in the first half of the eighteenth century, particularly in France and in circles under French influence such as the courts of German princes, the libertine spirit of Bussy-Rabutin and his like was in vogue. Freed by the restraint imposed upon court life during Louis XIV's last years, the aristocracy sought stimulus and enjoyment in the literary salons of the Duchess of Maine and of Madame de Lambert. Petronius was a welcome guest, and the more salacious of his episodes, particularly the amorous encounter of Polyaenos and Circe, were recited with gusto.

But the still recent discovery of the *Cena* provided a new inspiration. Why not put on a real Trimalchio's feast? And so we hear that at Saint-Cloud, a wealthy and worldly cleric, the Abbé de Margon, spent no less than 30,000 livres in providing such an entertainment at which the Regent himself was the guest of honor. Some years previously, in 1701, at the court of Hanover, Count Charles-Maurice, the Electress' nephew, had played Trimalchio at a feast in which no detail of Petronius was omitted. Leibnitz gave a full description, for he was present, to the Princess Louise of Hohenzollern in a letter dated February 25, 1702.[27] Trimalchio made his entry reclining on cushions, accompanied by deafening music, the authentic fantastic dishes were served, including the representation of the Zodiac and the astrological dissertation to follow. A refinement on the original was the spectacle of a giant chamber pot which followed Trimalchio everywhere. His last testament was recited amid universal groans, and the quarrel between Trimalchio and Fortunata (played by a Mlle von Poelnitz) was most realistic.

At the court of the francophile Frederick the Great of Prussia a similar feast was given in November, 1751.

Italy maintained a frozen silence. Not one translation of the whole *Satyricon* appeared there in the eighteenth century. Moreover, with the dawn of the Age of Reason, even the French ceased to be much entertained by our author, except in dramatic presentations of the Matron. We are passing into the age of critical editions and analytical commentaries of the classics, and Petronius becomes more the perquisite of the professional scholar. Original minds in search of inspiration tend to shy away from an author thus encumbered by a bulk of erudition, thus fenced in by a palisade of logical deduction and learned explanation. Most significant are the remarks of Voltaire, to our minds so kindred a spirit to Petronius, the style of whose *contes* so vividly recalls that of the Roman that we can scarcely understand that he did not acknowledge him as his master. The great French satirist seems to have had little regard for our author, whom he quotes rarely and, for the most part, inaccurately.[28] Perhaps Petronius showed too much Rabelaisian frenzy and disorderly extravagance for the disciplined eighteenth-century mind. Or perhaps simply Petronius and Voltaire were so alike in genius that the one repelled the other.

The idealistic spirit of the French Revolution was hostile to our author, and several editions of him which had been prepared in the last years of the century were suppressed as liable to have a demoralizing effect on the public. Some people were irritated by the Nodot forgeries which editors persisted in printing throughout the eighteenth century. A 1799 edition coincided with the appearance of a new fake, purporting to derive from a very old manuscript of St. Gall, a fragment to complete the scabrous Chapter 26 of the *Satyricon.* The author of this imposture was José Marchena, a Spaniard serving with the French Army of the Rhine. Some critics were deceived, and the eventual confession of Marchena must have done discredit to Petronius in this serious-minded age.

IX *Modern Times*

With the nineteenth century, creative literature, unless it be in the art of the translator, says good-bye to Petronius, except for the Matron's story. He is familiar to many poets and novelists who quote him or allude to him now and then, generally as the author of the *Cena,* the creator of Trimalchio. But he cannot be said to have real influence on the literary output of the time.

An exception to this is perhaps Anatole France, enthusiastic amateur of the classics, whose *Rôtisserie de la reine Pédauque* (1893) is something of a *satyricon* in its episodic structure. Certainly France read and reread his Petronius and absorbed not a little of his style, but he is perhaps still more indebted to Apuleius, in whose romancing he took special delight. But he shared with the Arbiter his pleasure at the passing spectacle of foolish mankind embroiled in distracting passions and preoccupations.[29]

The great service rendered by this scientific century was the establishment of a sound text of Petronius, upon which accurate commentary could for the first time be based. Italy still lagged behind, but the German Franz Buecheler grappled with the problem and produced in 1862 his major edition, the sure foundation for all subsequent work upon our author. It stirred the Italian Giovanni Cesareo to provide a brilliant and accurate translation of *Le Satire* in 1887. From then on, the Italians were well to the fore in research on their countryman, as they have continued to be to this day, concerning themselves especially with the problems connected with the date of Petronius and the precise locale of the *Cena* (See Bibliography).

With the numerous critical editions, commentaries, dissertations on language, lexicons, and translations of Petronius which abound in the nineteenth and twentieth centuries we are not here concerned, as they are not strictly a part of his literary influence. The more important will be listed further on. Our tale is virtually completed. It remains only to speak of a curious resurgence of the Arbiter in completely new guise at the dawn of our own century.

Henryk Sienkiewicz (1846–1916),[30] who had studied philology at Warsaw University and remained throughout his life an ardent lover of the classical world, began his career as a newspaper correspondent and journalist. But he soon made his name as a historical novelist and achieved fame with the trilogy *With Fire and Sword, The Flood,* and *Pan Michael,* published between 1884 and 1887, novels dealing with Poland's heroic aspirations towards independence in the second half of the seventeenth century when threatened by anarchical government at home and constant invasion from her neighbors. These conditions still prevailed in the latter part of the nineteenth century in a country divided between Prussian, Austrian, and Russian domination. Sienkiewicz aimed by his writings to keep alive Poland's national ideals and traditions and to preserve the nation's youth from demoralization. His brilliant evocative powers and his passionate patriotism won the gratitude of his fellow countrymen. In 1905 he received the Nobel Prize for literature.

In 1896 appeared *Quo Vadis?*, an immediate success, translated simultaneously into English and French in 1900 and thereafter into more than thirty other languages. The setting of this novel is the Rome of Nero, its theme the triumph of Christianity. In the sufferings of the early martyrs at the hands of their pagan persecutors, backed by the might of imperial Rome, the author saw an inspiring parallel to the plight of his compatriots, who indeed took the novel to their hearts, as did the rest of the world. In spite of the book's highly sensual and occasionally almost sadistic atmosphere it found pride of place in many a devoutly Christian home.

The presentation of the background, events and characters is on the whole realistic to the utmost degree, and Sienkiewicz steeped himself in Tacitus to achieve it. The title is derived from the legend of Saint Peter's encounter, when fleeing from Nero's persecution at Rome, with Christ upon the Appian Way, of Whom he asked "Quo Vadis?" (whither goest Thou?), receiving the reply "To Rome, to be crucified anew, for thou dost abandon my sheep." The incident is commemorated in the chapel of Domine quo vadis on this same Appian Way.

Petronius is of course one of the principal characters of the novel which in fact opens with the description of his rising at midday after a prolonged banquet with Nero. In the amplitude of details which the fictitious account gives of the Arbiter, essential truth is maintained, so that Sienkiewicz may be taken as an admirable elaboration of Tacitus. Nor is there any reason to suppose that the Pole had any need to seek inspiration from predecessors who had treated of the theme of imperial Roman decadence in their novels. We do not know if he was sufficiently versed in English and French to have profited from Bulwer-Lytton's *Last Days of Pompeii* or from Chateaubriand's *Martyrs*.

However, it must be admitted that Sienkiewicz shows little acquaintance with the actual *Satyricon,* which he indeed mentions in his second chapter, not as a court entertainment, but as a little work its author would have kept as secret as possible.[31] Trimalchio's name is mentioned on the same occasion and only once again in the whole novel. Nowhere is the Pole in debt to the *Satyricon,* and we are at liberty to wonder if in fact he had read the work, for surely in that case he would have found much detail, at least in the *Cena,* with which to adorn his recital and to increase its verisimilitude. How true it is that the modern world, as far as concerns the general reader, owes its knowledge of Petronius far more to Tacitus than to the Arbiter's own work. This state of affairs the brisk modern translation of Professor Arrowsmith will do much to remedy.[32]

In one trait particularly does Sienkiewicz' Petronius notably differ from the Arbiter as depicted by Tacitus and discerned by the reader of the *Satyricon*. He is much intrigued by the new Christian cult and ponders frequently upon its teachings. Inevitably, in the novel, he is in sympathy with the feelings of his intimate friend Vinicius, who embraces the faith of his beloved Lygia. But we can hardly subscribe to Sienkiewicz' portrait of him patiently and seriously listening to Paul of Tarsus at his friend's house (Chapter 39) and, although he rejects the new message of Christian love and the eternal recompense, being obviously moved and somehow impressed. He even admits the possibility that his soul may, after death, meet up with those of the two lovers (Chapter 72). This is most unlike the Petronius who in the *Satyricon* takes the opportunity to deride in gross burlesque at least the non-Roman forms of religious belief. It is true that he does not mention the Christians, and it is absurd to believe, as some have done, that Trimalchio's anxiety at the crowing of a cock (*Satyricon,* Chapter 74) is a parody of Peter's betrayal of Christ, or that the condition for Eumolpus' legatees in Chapter 141, whereby they must devour his body, is a satire on the Last Supper. The ancient Milesian Tale of the Matron cannot possibly parody the Resurrection, as has fantastically been alleged.

The truth must surely be that, although Petronius was fully aware of the Christians and a witness to their persecution, he was completely indifferent to their fate.

Quo Vadis? brought our Petronius to the silver screen. The Italians made a mighty presentation of it in 1912. The film was bought by the Americans and enjoyed a record-breaking run of twenty-two weeks at the Astor Theatre in New York in 1913. It caused Hollywood furiously to think, and D. W. Griffith's *The Birth of a Nation* was the outcome (1914), launching the American motion-picture industry upon the super-spectacle "feature" film. The 1930's again saw a *Quo Vadis?* and the latest version was by Metro-Goldwyn-Mayer in glorious technicolor in 1951 (Peter Ustinov as Nero, Leo Genn as Petronius). Thus was it hoped to combat the threat of television.[33]

X *To Sum Up*

The influence of Petronius lies in the realm of appreciation rather than of creative indebtedness. The *Satyricon* is too individual a work to lend itself with real success to direct imitation. It has been appreciated throughout the centuries with more genuine affection than that given to classical writings of much greater scope and importance. No work has greater literary merit within its appointed sphere. There is superb skill in the construction, narrative power, characterization, and language. Critics have for the most part praised these qualities wholeheartedly, whatever reservations they have had about its moral tone.

The chief defect of appreciation has been the failure to place the work in its true context. It has been regarded chiefly as a satire on the age of Nero and as such it has seemed to fall short of its purpose. The satire does not castigate, it condones, and traditional association of the author with Horace and Juvenal is puzzled by the fact. Petronius obviously loathes hypocrisy, the main characteristic of all his portrayals, but is he himself the complete hypocrite? Hardly, for he lacks the fervent sincerity which marks the type. He is neither a Sallust nor a Seneca.

He shows human nature at work, particularly in obedience to its strongest impulse, sexual desire. The clue is here, but the reader, even when he is not Baudelaire's *hypocrite lecteur*,[34] fails to see it, for he does not understand the tradition behind Petronius, the tradition which the young men of Rome knew and were anxious to preserve, the tradition of the Fauni and Satyroi, of the Fescennine revels and the Atellan farces, deliberately kept alive in the theatrical and musical schools of the *palaestrae*, in short the world of the *satyricos*. The ingredients of the *Satyricon*, poetry, rhetoric, and mime, were not recognized as the key to the essential nature and purpose of the work. They were still a part of the pagan tradition of John of Salisbury's century, but he was isolated in his understanding of them as one of the sole possessors of a Petronian manuscript in his time. After then, they were lost to the world, and modern scholarship is still searching for the origins of ancient popular humor and for the meaning of the satyr's function.

But the world through the ages has enjoyed Petronius. Saint-Evremond, Bussy-Rabutin, Anatole France, Sienkiewicz, and the

Hollywood producers have been well content with the Tacitean version of the Arbiter. Mercury, Priapus, Rome's versions of Dionysiac revelers, goat men and mime players have not concerned them in their appreciation. The decadent symbol of a decadent age has stirred their imaginations well enough. The not at all decadent and ever flourishing symbol of the phallos is best left alone. The satyric is the more secure, obscured by the satirist.

Notes and References

Chronology

1. Gilbert Bagnani, *Arbiter of Elegance* (Toronto, 1954), p. 56, suggests that our author was born about A.D. 20. To my mind, this date is a little too early for the following reason.

To place Petronius' birth in A.D. 20 is to make him seventeen years older than Nero, for the latter was born on December 15, A.D. 37.

We must bear in mind that the Arbiter was, if only for a brief period, an intimate friend and companion of Nero. From this it surely follows that he must have been young and energetic enough to participate in the entertainments of his master, including the banquets often prolonged throughout the night, followed by the escapades and practical jokes which sent forth bands of revelers into the streets of Rome to harass belated citizens and to commit what acts of vandalism took their fancy at such times (Suetonius, *Nero,* 26). We may in fact assume that the Arbiter was expected to organize such activity and to ensure its novelty and daring. A man seventeen years older than the protagonist for whom these revels were devised is hardly a becoming figure on the scene.

However, to give a certain measure of seniority to Petronius over Nero is to accord to him the necessary authority of experience in the art of living which would make his presence welcome and secure that deference which it is certain the emperor granted him.

Let us say then that the Arbiter was born about A.D. 27. This gives him ten years advantage over Nero, enough for worldly wisdom, not too much for the youth and zest required of him.

2. I would follow the Elder Pliny (*Natural History,* 37.7.20) who gives the *praenomen* Titus when relating an anecdote concerning our author. Pliny, born ca. A.D. 23, of similar social standing and wealth, almost certainly knew Petronius personally. The anecdote could not have been written more than a dozen years after the Arbiter's death, since Pliny himself perished in A.D. 79. The Medicean MS of the later books of Tacitus' *Annals* is untrustworthy as evidence for the *praenomen* Gaius (see H. Furneaux's edition, Vol. II [Oxford, 1907], p. 448, footnote to Book 16, chapter 17). Moreover, Tacitus' account dates from about A.D. 115.

3. Petronius may well have succeeded Tarquitius Priscus, governor in A.D. 59, who was condemned by the Senate in 61 for extortion (Tacitus, *Annals*, 14.46.1). His great wealth would commend him as being something of a guarantee that he would not behave as his predecessor had done.

4. Petronius Turpilianus, *consul ordinarius* in A.D. 61 together with Caesennius Paetus, was probably a brother of our author. He relinquished the office before time, when summoned to take command in Britain in place of Suetonius Paulinus, unsuccessful in dealing with the revolt of Boudicca. Titus possibly succeeded him for a few weeks as suffect consul until the new *ordinarius*, Calvisius Ruso, took office on March 1. The fact that he would only be thirty-four (if born A.D. 27) would not disqualify him for a purely honorific post, the mark of Nero's favor. It is reasonable to place his consulship not later than A.D. 61, for by 62 his enemy Tigellinus was established in the emperor's favor as Prefect of the Praetorian Guard, an event which must have precipitated the decline of Petronius' influence.

Titus Petronius has no known cognomen. I think it likely that he was the son of Publius Petronius, also without cognomen, consul in A.D. 19 (but see Gilbert Bagnani, *op. cit.* p. 56; also J. P. Sullivan, *The Satyricon of Petronius* [London, 1968], p. 32). This would make him the great-grandson of Caius Petronius, Prefect of Egypt in 24 B.C., in which office he amassed the immense fortune of which our author had his share. The cognomen Turpilianus appears to have been borne by the younger sons of this branch of the *gens Petroniana* (see Pauly-Wissowa, *Real-Encyclopädie der classischen Altertumswissenschaft* [Stuttgart, 1894–], Vol. 19, col. 1193; 1197–99). In this case, our Titus would be the elder brother of Petronius Turpilianus, the consul whom he replaced in A.D. 61.

Chapter One

1. For archeological and sociological background material for the middle of the first century A.D., consult *The Cambridge Ancient History* (Cambridge, 1934), Vol. 10, The Augustan Empire 44 B.C.—A.D. 70, chapters 13 and 21; R. H. Barrow, *Slavery in the Roman Empire* (London, 1928); J. Carcopino, *Daily Life in Ancient Rome*, trans. by E. O. Lorimer (Harmondsworth, 1964); A. M. Duff, *Freedmen in the Early Roman Empire* (Oxford, 1928); T. Frank, *An Economic History of Rome* (Baltimore, 1927); H. Mattingly, *Roman Imperial Civilization* (London, 1957); M. Rostovtzeff, *The Social and Economic History of the Roman Empire* (Oxford, 1957); T. G. Tucker, *Life in the Roman World of Nero and St. Paul* (London, 1910); A. W. Van Buren, *A Companion to the Study of Pompeii and Herculaneum* (Rome, 1933).

2. Tacitus, *Annals*, 15, 54–56.
3. Pauly-Wissowa, *Real-Encyclopädie, s.v.* Ofonius Tigellinus.
4. Sextus Afranius Burrus, favorite of Agrippina, Prefect of the Pretorian Guard under Claudius and Nero. Was Nero's tutor with Seneca. Died A.D. 62.
5. J. P. Sullivan, *op. cit.*, p. 32, suggests A.D. 64.
6. *The Oxford Classical Dictionary* (Oxford, 1953), p. 827.
7. For echoes of Seneca's writings in Petronius and perhaps deliberate parody, see J. P. Sullivan, *op. cit.*, pp. 129–38, 193–213.

Chapter Two

1. Codex Bernensis 357, copied at Auxerre in the ninth century. For details, see Konrad Müller, *Petronii Arbitri Satyricon* (Munich, 1961), p. VII.
2. For the expression *satyrica fabula* see H. Keil, ed. *Grammatici Latini* (Leipzig, 1857), I, 490.2, 18 and 491.3; *satyricum metrum, ibid.* VI, 151.26; *satyricum stylum,* VI, 81, 37; *satyrici chori,* VI, 99.19.
3. See J. P. Sullivan, *op. cit.*, Chapter IV, "Satire in the *Satyricon*."
4. E.g., Horace, *Epistles,* II, 1.139 ff.: *agricolae prisci, fortes parvoque beati,/condita post frumenta levantes tempore festo/corpus et ipsum animum spe finis dura ferentem,/—Tellurem porco, Silvanum lacte piabant.*
5. On Satyrs and Satyr plays, see H. J. Rose, *Handbook of Greek Mythology* (London, 1928), pp. 156 ff.; Pauly-Wissowa, *Real-Encyclopädie, s.v. satyros;* W. H. Roscher, ed., *Lexikon der griechischen und römischen Mythologie* (Leipzig, 1884–1937) *s.v.;* C. A. Van Rooy, *Studies in Classical Satire and Related Literary Theory* (Leiden, 1965), pp. 144–85.
6. See M. Bieber, *History of the Greek and Roman Theater* (Princeton, 1961), pp. 10–11.
7. E.g., Horace, *Ars Poetica,* 225, *satyri dicaces;* 233, *satyris—protervis;* Pliny, *Epistles* 9.17, *nequaquam me delectat, si quid molle a cinaedo, petulans a scurra, stultum a morione profertur.*
8. On the relationship between *satura* and *satyros,* see C. A. Van Rooy, *op. cit.*, pp. 136 ff.
9. For the Latin text, see Diomedes, *Ars Grammatica,* III, in H. Keil, *op. cit.* I, 485, 30 ff.
10. *The Oxford Classical Dictionary,* p. 316.
11. On the *palaestra,* home of the theater arts and in many ways the ancient equivalent of a modern university, see Ch. Daremberg and E. Saglio, *Dictionnaire des Antiquités grecques et romaines* (Paris, 1877–1919), *s.v.*
12. H. Keil, *op. cit.* VI, 153.

13. For examples, see Helen Waddell, *Medieval Latin Lyrics* (London, 1964); *The Wandering Scholars* (London, 1962).

14. On the mime and comedy situations, see J. P. Sullivan, *op. cit.*, pp. 219 ff.

15. H. Keil, *op. cit.* I, 482, 27.

16. Cf. Marius Victorinus in H. Keil, *op. cit.* VI, 151, 26.

17. Modern scholars are divided in opinion as to whether saturnians should be treated metrically or in terms of accentual rhythm. See D. S. Raven, *Latin Metre* (London, 1965), pp. 34–36, and R. G. Tanner, "The Arval Hymn and Early Latin Verse," *Classical Quarterly*, New Series XI, 2 (1961), pp. 216 ff.

18. *The Oxford Classical Dictionary*, p. 611 (Novel, Greek).

Chapter Three

1. For a recent "reconstruction" of the *Satyricon*, see J. P. Sullivan, *op. cit.*, chapter 2.

2. Alfons Hilka and Otto Schumann, eds., *Carmina Burana* Vols. 1–3 (Heidelberg, 1930, 1941).

3. The Elder Pliny (*Natural History*, 37.7.20) relates the story that Titus Petronius the consular, when about to die through the ill will of Nero, broke a vessel made of *murra* which he had purchased for 300,000 sesterces, in order to deprive the emperor of the use of it for his own table.

4. On the origins of drama at Rome and the part played by the young men about town in its conservation, see Livy, VII.2.

5. *The Oxford Classical Dictionary*, p. 747.

6. See J. M. G. M. Brinkhoff, *Woordspeling bij Plautus* (Nijmegen, 1935).

7. Some critics have taken seriously Hermeros' remark, "You are a Roman knight? Well, I'm a king's son, but I preferred to become a Roman citizen rather than to pay taxes as a foreigner." Cases like this were not unknown. Claudius' freedman Pallas (Tacitus, *Annals*, 12,53) was of royal stock, as also Nero's mistress Acte (Tacitus, *Annals*, 13,12). But modern scholars conclude that we cannot take the remark literally.

8. On the various factions ("Blues," "Greens," etc.) at the chariot races, see Daremberg-Saglio, *op. cit.*, I.2,1198 f. (circus, factions).

9. The ceremony was known as the *depositio barbae*, on which see Daremberg-Saglio, *op. cit.*, I.1,669 (*barba*).

10. Particularly in Plautus, Horace, and Cicero. The *locus classicus* on *scurrilia* is Cicero, *De Oratore*, II, 216–290, and see also P. Lejay, *Oeuvres d'Horace* (Paris, 1911) pp. 551 ff.

11. Danae—mother of Perseus by Zeus (Jupiter) who visited her in

a shower of gold when she was imprisoned in a bronze tower by her father Acrisius. See *The Oxford Classical Dictionary*, p. 667 (Perseus).

Chapter Four

1. See, however, J. P. Sullivan, *op. cit.*, chapter 3, "The Choice of Form."

2. See Florence Baldwin, *The Bellum Civile of Petronius* (New York, 1911). For an examination of Petronius' supposed critique of Lucan, see J. P. Sullivan, *op. cit.*, pp. 165–86.

3. For the life and work of Vincent of Beauvais, see *Encyclopaedia Britannica s.v.*

4. Anthony Rini *Petronius in Italy from the 13th Century to the Present Time* (New York, 1937).

5. H. Keil, *op. cit.*, VI, 399: *agnoscere haec potestis,/cantare quae solemus:/'Memphitides puellae/sacris deum paratae.'*

6. *Ibid.*, VI, 153: *metrum erit anacreontion, siquidem eo frequentissime usus sit, sed et apud nos plerique, inter quos Arbiter Satyricon ita 'triplici—orbem.'*

7. For Sidonius Apollinaris, see *The Oxford Classical Dictionary*, p. 837. He refers to Petronius as votary of Priapus in his 23rd Carmen: *'et te Massiliensium per hortos/sacri stipitis, Arbiter, colonum /Hellespontiaco parem Priapo.'*

8. In imperial and later times many of the pithy sayings of Publilius' characters were gathered together and amplified with material from other sources to provide books of proverbial wisdom for school use. The *Dicta Catonis* is a similar compilation. See J. Wight Duff and A. M. Duff, eds., *Minor Latin Poets* (Cambridge, Mass., 1934), pp. 15–111; 592–629.

9. For an account of this and other *florilegia* of the 12th–14th centuries, see B. L. Ullmann, "Petronius in the medieval florilegia," *Classical Philology,* 25 (1930), pp. 11 ff.

10. Clement C. I. Webb, ed., *Joannis Saresberiensis Policraticus,* 2 vols. (Oxford, 1909).

11. See Webb, *op. cit.*, vol. 2, Index Auctorum.

12. Shakespeare, *As You Like It,* Act 2, Scene 7. Montaigne also echoes Petronius in *Essais,* III, Chapter 10 (De Mesnager sa Volonté): "La plupart de nos vacations sont farcesques—mundus universus exercet histrioniam."

13. *The Oxford Classical Dictionary*, p. 673. See Alice Brenot, ed., *Phèdre* (Paris, 1924), where the fable is listed as No. 118 *Vidua et Miles* (Perotti's Appendix No. 13).

14. On the possible oriental origin of the Matron's story, see E. Paratore, *Il Satyricon di Petronio* (Florence, 1933), vol. 2, pp. 354

ff. Also E. Griesbach, *Die Wanderung der treulosen Witwe durch die Weltliteratur* (Berlin, 1886).

15. C. Alvaro, *Il Novellino* (Milan, 1945); E. Storer, *Il Novellino. The Hundred Old Tales* (New York, 1925).

16. For a concise account, see *Encyclopaedia Britannica, s.v.* Seven Wise Masters.

17. See Karl Warnke, ed., *Die Fabeln der Marie de France, Bibliotheca Normannica,* vol. 6 (Paris, 1898).

18. See Thomas Marc Parrott, *The Plays and Poems of George Chapman* (London, 1914).

19. For Pierre Mainfray, see H. C. Lancaster, *A History of French Dramatic Literature in the Seventeenth Century* (Baltimore, 1929), Part I, Vol. I, pp. 115 ff.

20. Paul Alexis and others, *Les Soirées de Médan* (Paris, 1926).

21. The saintly seventeenth-century author of devotional works, Jeremy Taylor, knew his Petronius well. He recalls Eumolpus "composing verses in a desperate storm" in a famous passage on life after death in his *Holy Dying* (1651). Ben Jonson has many echoes of our author, although the best known, which begins "Doing a filthy pleasure is, and short:/And done, we straight repent us of the sport" (*The Under-wood,* 88) is a rendering of *Foeda est in coitu et brevis voluptas,* etc., a fragment perhaps wrongly attributed to Petronius. See A. Ernout, *Pétrone, le Satiricon* (Paris, 1950), fragment 54, p. 201.

22. See *The Cambridge History of English Literature* (Cambridge, 1907–16), Vol. IX, chapter 10.

23. No recent edition of Barclay's *Satyricon* exists. For an account of the various editions and translations which have been made, none of which is readily available, see Jules Dukas, *Étude Bibliographique et Littéraire sur le Satyricon de Jean Barclay* (Paris, 1880). On Barclay's work in general, see *The Cambridge History of English Literature,* Vol. IV, pp. 253 ff.

24. For a detailed account of the discovery of the Traù MS, see Stephen Gaselee, *A Collotype Reproduction of that Portion of Cod. Paris, 7989 commonly called the Codex Traguriensis which contains the Cena Trimalchionis of Petronius* (Cambridge, 1915), pp. 1–9.

25. For an account of these editions, see Albert Collignon, *Pétrone en France* (Paris, 1905), p. 88, and Anthony Rini, *op. cit.,* p. 90.

26. See Anthony Rini, *op. cit.,* p. 99.

27. See Albert Collignon, *op. cit.,* p. 88, and Ludwig Friedländer, *Cena Trimalchionis* (Leipzig, 1906), p. 15, where the letter is reproduced in full.

28. For references to Petronius in Voltaire's letters, see Theodore Besterman, ed., *Voltaire's Correspondence* (Geneva, 1953–64), Vol. 99, col. 126. Remarks which seem to echo Voltaire's own are those of

Paul Desforges-Maillard in a letter dated 1752, in which he states that Petronius' novel does not belong to the time of Nero, but is the work of a voluptuary and dilettante of the time of the late empire. See Besterman, *op. cit.*, Vol. 21, Letter 4358.

29. For France's devotion to the spirit of the Milesian genre, see Barry Cerf, *Anatole France. The Regeneration of a Great Artist* (London, 1927), pp. 258–264.

30. On Sienkiewicz, see *Encyclopaedia Britannica, s.v.;* Monica M. Gardner, *The Patriot Novelist of Poland, Henryk Sienkiewicz* (London, 1926), and Mieczyslaw Giergielewicz, *Henryk Sienkiewicz* (New York, 1968).

31. " 'Here is a gift for thee' said he [Petronius]. 'Thanks!' answered Vinicius. Then, looking at the title, he inquired, ' "Satyricon"? Is this something new? Whose is it?' 'Mine. But I do not wish to go in the road of Rufinus, whose history I was to tell thee, nor of Fabricius Veiento; hence no one knows of this, and do thou mention it to no man.' " From Chapter Two of *Quo Vadis?* in Jeremiah Curtin's translation (London, 1900).

32. William Arrowsmith, *The Satyricon* (New York, 1959).

33. See Paul Rotha, *The Film Till Now* (London, 1960), pp. 72, 150.

34. "Hypocrite lecteur, mon semblable, mon frère," often quoted last line of the poem *Au Lecteur* which prefaces *Les Fleurs du Mal*. A good modern edition is Jacques Crépet et Georges Blin, eds., Charles Baudelaire, *Les Fleurs du Mal* (Paris, 1942).

Selected Bibliography

1. Editions

The first edition of the then known fragments of Petronius was compiled about 1482 by Francesco dal Pozzo (Puteolanus) and printed at Milan. A similar edition was produced at Venice in 1499. In 1565 Johannes Sambucus' Antwerp edition added new material, while that of Pierre Pithou, Paris 1577, made use of the important Berne codex. The *Cena Trimalchionis* was first published from the Traù MS at Padua in 1664. Particularly important are the two editions of Peter Burman (Utrecht 1709, Amsterdam 1743), providing a fulsome commentary compiled from the notes of distinguished scholars like Heinsius, Dousa, and Scheffer.

The best account of the numerous editions prior to that of Buecheler is given in Rini (see below).

The following is a list in chronological order of the principal modern editions.

BUECHELER, FRANZ. *Petronii Arbitri satirarum reliquiae*. Berlin: Weidmann, 1862. Lays the foundation of modern Petronian scholarship and forms the basis of all subsequent studies and editions.

FRIEDLÄNDER, LUDWIG. *Petronii Cena Trimalchionis*. Leipzig. S. Hirzel, 1891, 1906. Text and German translation. Useful introduction and notes.

WATERS, WILLIAM E. *Cena Trimalchionis*. New York; B. H. Sanborn, 1902, 1917. School edition with introduction and useful notes.

LOWE, W. D. *Cena Trimalchionis*. Cambridge: Deighton Bell, 1905. Translation with critical and explanatory notes.

HERAEUS, WILHELM. *Petronii Cena Trimalchionis*. Heidelberg: Carl Winter, 1909, 1939. Includes a selection of Pompeian inscriptions.

HESELTINE, MICHAEL. *Petronius*. Loeb Classical Library, New York: Macmillan, 1913. Valuable bibliography, especially for earlier editions.

ERNOUT, ALFRED. *Pétrone. Le Satiricon*. Paris: Les Belles Lettres, 1922, 1931, 1950. Best critical edition since Buecheler. Excellent French translation.

SEDGWICK, W. B. *The Cena Trimalchionis of Petronius.* Oxford: Clarendon Press, 1925, 1950. Excellent for class use.

SAGE, EVAN T. *Petronius. The Satiricon.* New York: The Century Co., 1929. Useful notes and bibliography.

MAIURI, AMEDEO. *La Cena di Trimalchione.* Naples: Pironti, 1945. Useful for archeological details and illustrations.

MARMORALE, ENZO V. *Petronii Arbitri Cena Trimalchionis.* Florence: La Nuova Italia, 1947. The best modern commentary, with extensive bibliography.

SCHMECK, HELMUT. *Petronii Cena Trimalchionis.* Heidelberg: Carl Winter, 1954. Text, apparatus, good bibliography.

ARROWSMITH, WILLIAM. *The Satyricon.* New York: Mentor Classics, 1959, 1963. Excellent, colloquial translation. Useful notes.

MÜLLER, KONRAD. *Petronii Arbitri Satyricon.* Munich: Ernst Heimeran, 1961. Important new edition and apparatus. Authoritative introduction (in Latin) on textual tradition.

SULLIVAN, JOHN P. *Petronius, The Satyricon and the Fragments.* Baltimore: Penguin Books, Inc., 1965. It is fascinating to compare this with William Arrowsmith's rendering for Mentor Classics (listed above). Both are splendid, racy translations in modern idiom. Sullivan's Introduction and Notes are particularly good.

MÜLLER, KONRAD and WILHELM EHLERS. *Petronius Satyricon. Schelmengeschichten.* Tusculum Series. Munich: Ernst Heimeran, 1965. Text and German translation. Important notes on textual tradition and on Petronius and his work.

2. Important Works of Reference

Articles and Notes on Petronius are listed year by year in *L'Année Philologique,* Paris: Les Belles Lettres.

AUERBACH, ERICH. *Mimesis; the Representation of Reality in Western Literature.* Princeton: University Press, 1953. See Chapter 2, "Fortunata," on Petronius as an interpreter of reality through literary imitation. He is the most "modern" realist in antique literature, but his realism is given comic treatment as applied to scenes of low life, in obedience to the convention of his day.

BAGNANI, GILBERT. *Arbiter of Elegance.* Toronto: University Press, 1954. Thorough examination of the evidence for the date and authorship of the *Satyricon.* Amusing and imaginative "biography" of Petronius.

BALDWIN, FLORENCE. *The Bellum Civile of Petronius.* New York: Columbia University Press, 1911. Edition, translation, and ample commentary. Good introduction.

BALSDON, J. P. V. D. *Roman Women.* London: The Bodley Head, 1962. Includes portraits of Messalina, Agrippina, and other notable women of the Neronian age. Also deals with the fictional characters of Petronius. Valuable background material.

BISHOP, JOHN. *Nero: The Man and the Legend.* New York: A. S. Barnes, 1964. Stimulating, readable modern account of the subject, giving new and original viewpoints of Nero's complex character.

BROWNING, ROBERT. "The Date of Petronius," *Classical Review* 63 (1949), pp. 12–14, 28–29. Argues against Marmorale's dating of Petronius at the end of the second century A.D. and supports the traditional Neronian date. Criticizes Marmorale's methods in *La Questione Petroniana*. Bari: Laterza, 1948.

CARCOPINO, JEROME. *Daily Life in Ancient Rome.* New Haven: Yale University Press, 1940. Most valuable for background material.

COLLIGNON, ALBERT. *Pétrone en France.* Paris: Fontemoing, 1905. Detailed account of Petronius' influence in France and of the various editions of his work.

COURTNEY, E. "Parody and Literary Allusion in Menippean Satire," *Philologus* 106 (1962), pp. 86 ff. Explains the author's view that Petronius' work is a parody of the novel genre. The Menippean form is the natural vehicle for such parody.

DUFF, ARNOLD M. *Freedmen in the Early Roman Empire.* Oxford: Clarendon Press, 1928. Exhaustive study of the freedman condition. Valuable in assessing the verisimilitude of Petronius' *Cena.*

GAGÉ, JEAN. *Les Classes Sociales dans l'Empire Romain.* Paris: Payot, 1964. A good modern study of the subject. Chapters 4, 5, and 7 are of particular relevance.

GASELEE, STEPHEN. *A collotype reproduction of that portion of codex Paris. 7989 which contains the Cena Trimalchionis.* Cambridge: University Press, 1915. Valuable introduction, with detailed account of the discovery of the Traù MS.

MARMORALE, ENZO V. *La Questione Petroniana.* Bari: Laterza, 1948. Discussion of authorship, date, setting and language of the *Satyricon.*

NELSON, H. L. W. *Petronius en zijn vulgair Latijn.* Alphen: J. M. Haasbeck, 1947. Detailed study of the language of the *Cena*, with summary in English.

PARATORE, ETTORE. *Il Satyricon di Petronio.* Florence: Felice Le Monnier, 1933. Tedious to read (657 pages), but deals exhaustively with many aspects of Petronian problems.

PERROCHAT, PAUL. *Pétrone, Le Festin de Trimalcion.* Paris: Presses Universitaires de France, 1962. Extremely useful commentary which summarizes most of the work done on Petronius to date.

RINI, ANTHONY. *Petronius in Italy from the 13th century to the Present Time.* New York: Cappabianca Press, 1937. Most valuable for

Petronius' influence in Italy and elsewhere, and also for full details of the MSS and editions.

ROSE, K. F. C. "The date of the Satyricon," *Classical Quarterly* 12 (1962), pp. 166–68. Argues for the Neronian date from name references in the *Satyricon*. Suggests that the *Bellum Civile* was published in May-July of A.D. 65.

———. "Time and Place in the *Satyricon*," *Transactions of the American Philological Association* 93 (1962), pp. 402 ff. Deals with the possible locality of the *Cena*, the year and the season of the action of the *Satyricon*. Argues that Petronius probably gave the name of his *Graeca urbs* in some portion of the work now lost. Favors Puteoli in August. Such precisions would be in accordance with Petronius' realism.

ROSTOVTZEFF, M. *The Social and Economic History of the Roman Empire*, 2nd Edn. Oxford: Clarendon Press, 1957. Valuable background material on e.g. Campania, Puteoli, landowners, freedmen, commerce, etc.

SCHNUR, H. C. "Recent Petronian Scholarship (1940–56)," *Classical Weekly* 50 (1957), pp. 133–36; 141–43.

———. "The Economic Background of the *Satyricon*," *Latomus* 18 (1959), pp. 790 ff. Convincing arguments from the economic background for the Neronian date.

SEGEBADE, J. and E. LOMMATZSCH. *Lexicon Petronianum*. Leipzig: Teubner, 1898.

SOCHATOFF, A. F. "The Purpose of Petronius' *Bellum Civile*: a Reexamination," *Transactions of the American Philological Association* 93 (1962), pp. 449 ff. Summarizes the arguments for and against the notion that the *Bellum* is merely a parody and critique of Lucan. Traces briefly the history of the *Bellum* tradition and shows various possible motives for its composition.

STEFENELLI, ARNULF. *Die Volkssprache im Werk des Petron*. Stuttgart: Braumüller, 1962. Of interest to students of Romance philology.

SULLIVAN, JOHN P. *The Satyricon of Petronius*. London: Faber and Faber, and Bloomington; Indiana University Press, 1968. Excellent full-length literary study, the first in English. Resumes the evidence for date and authorship and essays a reconstruction which does much to clarify our understanding of the work. Stimulating chapters on Petronius' satiric intentions, his literary criticisms, parodies, and humor. Of particular interest is Sullivan's exploration of sexual themes in the *Satyricon*. Valuable bibliography and general index.

SYME, RONALD. *Tacitus*. Oxford: Clarendon Press, 1958. Essential background material. Suggests our author may be Titus Petronius Niger. See pp. 387 (note), 743.

VREESE, J. G. W. M. DE. *Petron 39 und die Astrologie*. Amsterdam: H. J. Paris, 1927. Fascinating investigation of the astrological details in Chapter 39 of the *Satyricon*.

Index

DATE DUE
